# God's Word To Pastors

## Understanding & Strengthening The Relationship Between The Pastor & His Congregation

*Bob Yandian*

P. O. Box 471692
Tulsa, OK 74147-1692

Unless otherwise noted, all scripture quotations
are from the King James Version of the Bible.


*God's Word To Pastors*
*Understanding & Strengthening The Relationship*
*Between The Pastor & His Congregation*
ISBN 1-880089-05-X
Copyright © 1992 by
Bob Yandian
P. O. Box 55236
Tulsa, OK 74155-1236


Published by:
Pillar Books & Publishing Company
P. O. Box 471692
Tulsa, OK 74147-1692
United States of America


Cover design & book production by:
sigma graphics, ltd.
Broken Arrow, OK
918-455-1072

# Table Of Contents

# Acknowledgements

SPECIAL THANKS goes to Elizabeth Sherman, my editor, through whose hands God works "special miracles." She has the difficult task of making me sound good in a book.

# Introduction

THE PASTOR OF THE LOCAL CHURCH today has many voices crying out to him, from both the natural world and the Christian world. And, as First Corinthians 14:10 tells us, "...none of them is without signification." Every voice is important.

As a pastor, I know that books by other pastors and ministers can bring great insight into the ministry and help us to avoid some of the pitfalls. I also know that much can be learned from secular books on time management and business administration, books written by successful business executives.

Most Christians view the ministry as being all spiritual, but there are many practical aspects of ministry as well. Often, we look to the Bible only for the spiritual side of ministry, then seek out practical books on the natural side. But the Bible is still the best source of information for natural as well as spiritual living.

*If a pastor were completely removed from all reading material but the Bible, his church could still be a great success, and his life could be balanced in both spiritual and natural areas.*

Second Peter 1:3 says that God "hath given unto us all things that pertain unto life (natural) and godliness (spiritual), through the knowledge of him...." The same Bible that tells us how we are joined to the Lord Jesus Christ also tells us how to be successful in being joined together in marriage.

The Word of God tells us how to have a full relationship with our Heavenly Father, but also gives principles to help us be successful parents. And not only does the Bible talk about faithfulness to God, but it also deals with honoring your employer.

Because we are citizens of two worlds, the kingdom of God and planet earth, the Holy Spirit was not slack in teaching us our responsibilities to each kingdom when He gave us the Word of God. He knows that ignorance of natural principles can lead to a spiritual disaster just as easily as ignorance of spiritual principles can lead to destruction in the natural.

When we face failure, we usually look for answers in fasting, longer prayer time, or possibly a promise we had overlooked or neglected to stand on from God's Word. But the problem could simply be a lack of time with our family or not delegating responsibility to others.

The "little foxes that spoil the vines" (see Song of Solomon 2:15) are often overlooked as we strive to carry out the vision God has given us, *but they are not overlooked in God's Word!* Since the Lord created both worlds, spiritual and natural, He saw to it that His Word to us contained wisdom for both realms in our lives.

Acts 20:17-38 is one of those special passages for pastors, in which Paul shares the practical side of the ministry with the pastors of Ephesus. The man who wrote the great letter to the Ephesian congregation, teaching them their wonderful spiritual heritage, now sits with their pastors to share the realities of the everyday challenges of pastoring.

In First Peter 5:1-6, Peter's counsel to the pastors of scattered Jewish believers closely parallels the godly wisdom Paul imparts in Acts, chapter 20. And there are several other scriptures that relate directly to how the pastor and the local church flow together in both spiritual things and natural things.

I'm certain that one of the main reasons the Holy Spirit included these passages of scripture in the Bible is that all ministers, but particularly pastors, are the favorite targets of Satan and his demon army. It is a great accomplishment for the devil to sidetrack a member of the congregation, but his greatest trophies are pastors he has managed to shipwreck.

Destruction of leadership leaves in its wake many more broken and confused followers. This is why the office of the pastor is always under such supernatural attack. If the enemy can eliminate the shepherd, he can scatter the flock and devour some of the sheep.

Discouragement, exhaustion, and frustration easily plague a pastor if he doesn't recognize and follow certain natural principles in the Word of God. It doesn't take intense spiritual revelation to come out of many of the devil's traps!

Satan's devices can be as simple as causing a minister to get his priorities out of line or tempting him to value the wrong things at the wrong time. Also, pastors are often guilty of not heeding the wisdom in their own sermons!

By the time Paul and Peter imparted this practical wisdom to pastors, they had endured many years of ministry. They had learned what works and what doesn't, what to do and what not to do. And the principles that they give to these ministers, if followed, will produce both longevity and joy in ministry for us today.

# Chapter One
# Paul Calls the First Pastors' Conference

**And from Miletus he sent to Ephesus, and called the elders of the church.**

**Acts 20:17**

PAUL WAS THE APOSTLE the Holy Spirit sent to establish the original church in Ephesus. He spent three years there, and during that time he saw one of the most tremendous revivals of his ministry. From this great revival, many local churches were raised up, and many pastors were raised up with them.

It has now been nearly two years since he was in Ephesus, and the Holy Spirit is sending Paul back to minister to those pastors. Therefore, in Acts 20:17-38, we have the very first recorded pastors' conference, as Paul calls for the pastors of Ephesus to join him in Miletus.

## The End Result of Revival

When Paul calls the pastors of Ephesus to come to Miletus, they have been "in the trenches" for many months since his sudden and dramatic departure from them in Acts 19. If you remember, a riot, led by the silver workers' union, had broken out in Ephesus, and Paul was forced to flee for his life.

The revival which had lasted nearly two years under Paul's apostleship had left the silver industry, one of Ephesus' main industries, in economic disaster. Small figures of Diana, which usually brought great amounts of money from her worshipers, were now sitting on store shelves, because people

1

throughout Ephesus and the whole continent of Asia had turned to the Lord Jesus Christ.

Since the craft of these silver idols was a major industry in Ephesus, Demetrius, the president of the silver union, assembled a union meeting of all the craftsmen and put the blame for their financial losses squarely on the shoulders of Paul (Acts 19:24-27).

During the course of this assembly, a religious and patriotic frenzy mounted until it spread out into the streets with the emotional outcry, "Great is Diana of the Ephesians" (Acts 19:28)! Inevitably, the mob deteriorated into a crowd of confused people, yelling and rioting without really knowing why they were there.

Out of control, the angry crowd rushed the home of two innocent friends of Paul and dragged them into the center of town. Paul wanted to save them, but the other disciples begged him not to get involved (Acts 19:29-31).

Paul was caught in the middle of a divided city. His greatest desire was to stay with the new converts and help the new churches become established, but concern for his own safety overruled his desire, and with an emotional good-bye he left for Macedonia (Acts 20:1).

After Paul's departure, the new churches had to stand on their own as the explosive situation in Ephesus continued. Months later, when Paul returned and asked them to meet him in Miletus (Acts 20:17), they were ready for some encouragement!

These pastors and ministers must have felt orphaned when Paul was rushed out of town during the riot at Ephesus. More importantly, their minds must have raced with the questions, "Is this the result of revival in a city? Does God bring a man like Paul here only to have him run out of town? And if God brings revival, can men end it? How can something begin in such power and end in such confusion?"

No doubt, many of these questions were also being asked by the pastors' congregations! "Where are the miracles now? Will we ever see special miracles like when the handkerchiefs and aprons of ministers caused disease and evil spirits to leave the sick and oppressed (Acts 19:11,12)?

"Will more of Satan's ministers be exposed, like the seven sons of Sceva (Acts 19:13-17)? Will we see more followers of the occult burn their books publicly as they acknowledge Jesus as their Lord and Savior (Acts 19:19)?"

These same questions are being asked by believers in America today. Will we see another Azusa Street, where the power of God was in such manifestation that the fire department arrived on several occasions to put out a fire that was not a natural fire, but a supernatural blaze of God's power and glory?

Will tremendous healings and miracles be front-page news again? Will denominational barriers crumble under the sovereign move of the Holy Spirit as they did in the charismatic movement?

Believers in America today are crying out for more revival, but is the conclusion of revival more revival? The answer is simple and obvious as we study the aftermath of the revival in Ephesus in Acts, chapter 20. The result of that revival was the establishing of local churches that turned their communities "right side up."

Nowhere in the Bible is there an example of perpetual revival. Revival produces many converts filled with zeal, but stability comes from growing up spiritually within the local church. Remember that our command was not to make *converts* of all nations, but *disciples* (Matthew 28:19,20).

A *disciple,* defined by Jesus in John 8:31,32, is "one who continues in God's Word." This definition is confirmed in the account of the Ephesus revival in Acts, chapter 19. After the mass conversions, miracles, healings, exposing of false ministers, and burning of occult literature, verse 20 states, "So mightily grew the word of God and prevailed."

After revival, Ephesus had a "Word" movement! Local churches were springing up to make disciples of converts by teaching the Word of God. *Revival is successful only through the growth of local assemblies, where the teaching of the Word of God brings stability to a congregation.*

Ephesus was divided by the gospel, but stabilized by the local church. The church of Ephesus went on to be one of the greatest of the ancient world. After the churches at Jerusalem and Antioch had both fallen into legalism, the church of Ephesus became the main center of world evangelism.

Timothy pastored the church of Ephesus during Paul's second imprisonment, and therefore Ephesus was the recipient of both of Paul's letters to Timothy. This church also became one of the largest in the ancient world, numbering in the tens of thousands.

The gospel shook Ephesus and Asia, but the church of Ephesus shook the world with the gospel!

## What About America?

In our own country, we have seen a tremendous hunger for the Word of God after the healing movement of the 1950's and the charismatic movement of the 1960's. Hunger for the Word of God causes the transition from revival to the birth of local churches.

Today, strong local churches are being established all across the nation, and as they preach and teach the Word of God to their people, these believers are transforming their communities.

Many of these churches have weekly crowds that outnumber the tent meetings and seminars of ten and twenty years ago. The hunger for God and His Word is being satisfied, and the needs of the people are being supernaturally met in the local church today.

Also, as revival moved across the nation in tents and seminars during the healing and charismatic movements, God began to raise up pastors who proclaimed, "Why should people have to go to a special meeting to hear the Word of God, to be healed, or to have their family restored? These blessings should be found in the local church!"

The Bible does not say, "Is there any sick among you, let him call for the elders of the tent or the seminar." There should be elders of the local church who know how to pray for healing (James 5:14).

Just like the church of Ephesus, the local church is ordained to be the focal point of evangelism into its community, and a hub of evangelism into the world as they support missionaries whom God raises up in their midst.

The other full-time ministry offices of apostles, prophets, evangelists, and teachers should also be members of a local church along with their families. A traveling ministry is stabilized when they have a home church praying for them and supporting them. It is not an accident that the time we live in is called the Church Age!

The local church is the visible, living example of the invisible universal Church, and Jesus said that "the gates of hell shall not prevail against it" (Matthew 16:18). While movements, ministries, and revivals come and go, the local church continues to survive. And I believe that local churches will be victorious and triumphant monuments to the power of God when Jesus returns.

## Pastors Need Pastoring, Too

Pastors teach, uplift, and encourage their congregations day after day, service after service, and week after week, but who encourages them? They have their treasure in an earthen vessel just like every other Christian, and after awhile, their vessel can become tired, discouraged, and even disoriented.

There are times when a pastor needs to get away to be pastored himself, just like those from Ephesus. That is why it is good to have pastors' conferences!

For those of you who are going into the ministry or are already in the ministry, it's good to take a break from the church once in awhile, to sit down with other pastors and find out that your problems are not unique, that you are not the only one facing certain situations.

As a minister, one of the most refreshing times comes when you fellowship with other ministers, when you talk and laugh and cry with them about all the things you are going through. You can sit in your church and think, "Boy, this is the most unusual problem. No one ever faced this problem!" But when you fellowship with others in the same field, you begin to discover that the devil is the same wherever you go, he pulls the same tricks on everyone – and ALL ministers are human!

I want you to note that, although Paul's conference was for the pastors at Ephesus, the conference was not held there, but in Miletus, which is a little town about thirty miles south of Ephesus. Besides the continued danger to his life in Ephesus, there is another reason why God had Paul call these pastors away from their churches for awhile.

Whenever there is a pastors' conference in Tulsa, which is where I pastor, I hardly ever attend. The ones I usually go to are out of town, because then I don't have any pressure to be at the church.

If I'm out of town, it's a lot harder for someone on my staff to call my hotel room or leave a message and say, "You have to meet with this person," or "We really need you here," or "Can you give this person a call as soon as possible?"

When I go to a conference away from home, I can attend all the meetings and hear all the speakers. I can give my full attention to receiving from God. So it was the wisdom of God that led Paul to bring the pastors of Ephesus away from their homes and their churches. In this way, they could truly rest from the challenges of the ministry, get to all the meetings of the conference, and get a fresh perspective as they enjoyed the company of other ministers.

What Paul shares with these pastors in the town of Miletus is as powerful and effective for us today as it was for the Ephesian pastors in the first days of the Church Age. Problems have not changed, because Satan and his demons are still the same. Nor have the answers changed, because "Jesus Christ is the same yesterday, today and forever" (Hebrews 13:8).

# Chapter Two
# Hold Nothing Back

And when they were come to him, he said unto them, Ye know, from the first day that I came into Asia, after what manner I have been with you at all seasons,

Serving the Lord with all humility of mind, and with many tears, and temptations, which befell me by the lying in wait of the Jews:

And how I kept back nothing that was profitable unto you, but have shewed you, and have taught you publicly, and from house to house...

Acts 20:18-20

THESE FOUR VERSES OF SCRIPTURE begin Paul's message to the elders of Ephesus. He has come to give them encouragement and instruction, to pour out all the knowledge and wisdom he can to help them accomplish what God has called them to do.

As an apostle, Paul also had functioned as pastor of the first church that began in Ephesus, and many of these pastors have come up directly under his leadership.

You see, the Holy Spirit may bring an apostle to start a church, and while the apostle temporarily serves as pastor to that church, God raises up the pastor from among the elders. Then the apostle will move on to begin another church, and the process begins again.

That is what Paul has done with many of these men. And, for the moment, Paul is speaking to them as a pastor to pastors, as the apostle who helped them grow up in the ministry.

## At All Seasons

Paul begins by saying, "Ye know, from the first day that I came into Asia, after what manner I have been with you at all seasons." "At all seasons" refers to the three years that Paul had spent with them, and that they have seen him at his best, and they have seen him at his worst!

The phrase "at all seasons" reminds us that our lives have times of rejoicing and times of sorrow, times of excitement and times of boredom, times of frustration and times of contentment. Just as the year brings different seasons, our lives contain changes and we change. The only One Who never changes is Jesus (Hebrews 13:8).

Therefore, Paul is instructing the pastors to be transparent with their people. Admit it when you make mistakes, and praise God and give Him glory when you have victories. Let them know that you go through seasons just like they go through seasons – but let them see the consistency of Jesus by being faithful in the Word of God while you go through these seasons.

No one is on top of it every single day – don't kid me! You might say, "Well, I'm believing I'm more than a conqueror, and I'm confessing it." Well, why are you confessing it? If you've already arrived, you wouldn't need to be confessing it, would you?

The point is, there are times when you are down and there are times when you are up, so don't give the impression that you're always up. If you do, you will discourage the people.

If the pastor is always "up there," the congregation will think they can never get up to his level. Aren't you glad to know that Jesus was tempted in all points as you are (Hebrews 4:15)? Even though He *didn't sin*, He still experienced everything you experience. And because of this, He can say to you, "I was right there, too, and I'll strengthen you to make it through this ordeal successfully."

Paul is saying to these pastors, "There were times when I came to preach to you and I was really on top of it, and there were times when I came and fell flat on my face. There were times when there was no anointing, or I was discouraged or upset.

"Pressures were on me from religious people, or the government. Money was low. But I'll tell you what, you saw me *at all seasons.* And I continued to preach and teach the Word regardless of what was going on in my life. I was as real out of the pulpit as I was in the pulpit, and I stayed faithful."

*Stay faithful!* That's one of the keys of the kingdom of God – faithfulness. (See my book, **Calling and Separation,** which discusses this principle in greater detail.) Paul is making the point that he lived a consistent life before these pastors. He's reminding these pastors that God doesn't reward you for staying "on top." He rewards you for being faithful, for being consistent in the Word of God.

In Philippians 3:13,14 Paul wrote, "Brethren, I count not myself to have apprehended: but this one thing I do, forgetting those things which are behind, and reaching forth unto those things which are before, I press toward the mark for the prize of the high calling of God in Christ Jesus."

It is good to let your congregation know that you haven't arrived yet, but in the face of every situation and every circumstance, whether good or bad, whether up or down, show yourself to be faithful at all seasons to study and feed them the Word of God.

## Grace Thinking

Paul continues with, "Ye know, from the first day that I came into Asia, after what manner I have been with you at all seasons, Serving the Lord with all *humility of mind."* Now, you may ask, "What is 'humility of mind'?" I call this "grace thinking." "Grace thinking" is getting rid of all thoughts of superiority, humbling yourself before God in order to see others the way He sees them.

There are always going to be people who irritate and frustrate you as you minister to or counsel them. If you choose the attitude of "humility of mind," or "grace thinking," you will obtain the grace from God that will enable you to continue to minister to them effectively and compassionately. But if you decide you're so much better than they are, you will grow more and more impatient and insensitive to them. So the Bible says to serve the Lord with "all humility of mind," or "grace thinking."

It's so important that, as a minister, you look at your people through the eyes of grace, through the eyes of love. And realize something: it's easy to get discouraged with people when they have to come back for spiritual help more than one time for the same thing, when they ask you the same questions week after week.

It's very easy to look at a person who is struggling with something you feel is so easy and say, "If you ever darken this door again..." or smile at them as they walk out the door and then think, "What a klutz!"

Now don't think that I haven't been tempted in this way! I'm human. There are times when people come in my office and I think, "Don't they know what the Word says?" It seems to me that they are overlooking the most simple verses in the Bible. But when "grace thinking" is working in my life, the Lord says, "How long did it take YOU to learn that?" Then I look at them through the eyes of grace.

How long did He have to put up with me in certain areas? How long did it take me to learn certain lessons? How many times did God have to pick me up for the same stupid mistake over and over again? Oh, how quickly we forget our own weaknesses when it comes to helping others! And how often do we overlook the fact that we have failed and God was there to pick us up, yet we demand perfection of everyone around us.

Paul is exhorting the pastors to look at their congregations through the same eyes of grace and love that the Lord Jesus Christ looks at them, to treat their people as Jesus treats them. Remember that His Word and His patience are what changed you, and it took time!

## With Many Tears

There are times in the ministry when you will experience hurt, pain, and the shedding of tears. There are several reasons for why we are brought to tears in the ministry, so do not be surprised by this. As a matter of fact, Paul told his friends, "Serving the Lord with all humility of mind, and *with many tears.*"

You say, "Why do tears come?" Very often it is because you find out what people are *really* like. Sometimes people put on big facades when they are in church. They have big smiles on their faces as they walk out the door, and they make great promises about what they're going to do for you – then you never hear from them again.

On other occasions people will tell you, "You're going to have a building program? I'll pledge! You need some chairs? I'll buy twenty of them!" You say, "Well, glory to God!" Then you see them from week to week, and you're thinking, "What about the pledge? What about the chairs?" And they just walk by and smile.

It's then that you have to say, "No! I can't think that!" You can't look at people through the eyes of their promises. Later on, you'll probably find out that what they promised was something they wanted to do, but in the end it was beyond their level of faith or ability to follow through.

You learn very quickly in the ministry that there is a lot of presumptuous talk within the church. You learn to take promises with a grain of salt. If they promise, don't get excited right away. Let them prove themselves.

New people can walk in and tell you this is the church they have been looking for. They tell you they will be back next week to join, and then you'll never see them again. Others will tell you when you first take over the church that you are the pastor they have been praying for. They will commit to helping in any area you need them, stay for two weeks, and never return!

Ironically, one of the most difficult times for the pastor is when the church begins to grow. Church growth is a blessing, but more blessing brings more responsibility and more problems! The most common complaints are, "Things aren't like they used to be. I used to know everybody. Now it seems so cold. Pastor used to come pray for me, but now he sends one of the counselors."

There are those members who cannot handle the change from a smaller building to a larger one. When people are crammed into the sanctuary, sitting in the aisles and standing around the back, the *excitement* of what seems to be a big crowd can be mistaken for a powerful *anointing!*

When you move into the new big building, all of a sudden there are empty seats and a lot of people who are unfamiliar (these are the rest of the congregation who had attended the other two morning services when you were in the old building). The pastor begins to hear things like, "There is no anointing on this building. The church has really changed since we moved. I don't recognize half the people here. Church is just not as powerful as it used to be."

What hurts most is when someone gets saved in the church, their family gets saved, and as they are faithful to the Word of God, you watch their lives turn around. They begin to look better, their family is happier and healthier, and then one day you notice they aren't in service.

After several Sundays pass and they haven't returned, you call them and ask how they are doing and why they haven't been to church. They reply, "The church has just gotten too big, Pastor. We are going to a smaller church where we can really feel a part of things." Later, you hear that they are having serious problems again because the church they are attending may be smaller, but the Word is not being taught, believed, or practiced.

As a church grows, the pastor has less one-on-one contact with the members. Because he cannot and should not do everything himself, he begins to delegate his authority in various areas to others. Some people are offended by this, even if he teaches the principle of delegation from the Word of God (see Chapter Five).

Unless the pastor prays for them, they are not satisfied that God has touched them. So they leave the church saying, "Well, the pastor has just gotten too big to minister to us." In reality, the church has gotten too big for the pastor to minister to them as a personal counselor, but he would have seen to it that they received what they needed from someone on staff or a capable volunteer.

It is ironic that a congregation will pray to reach their city for Jesus, that people will come and be saved, and when the church finally grows – they leave! However, the strain of church growth on a congregation is as old as the Church. In Acts 6:1 it says, "And in those days, *when the number of the disciples were multiplied, there arose a murmuring…"*

To appease those who were complaining, the apostles appointed deacons to minister to the people so that they could concentrate on the Word of God and prayer (the pastor's primary responsibilities). Most likely, the murmurers were probably some of those who had been shouting for joy in the upper room a few months before!

These are the "many tears" from *within* the church, but there can be tears from *outside* your church, as well. Paul refers to these tears when he writes: "Serving the Lord with all humility of mind, and with many tears, and temptations, *which befell me by the lying in wait of the Jews."*

The worst enemy to the gospel always has been and always will be religion. Because many people think that faith in Jesus Christ is "religion," I want to define this term before we go any further.

"Religion" is any counterfeit of or alternative to salvation and Christian living through faith in Jesus Christ. True Christianity is not religion; it is an intimate relationship between God and man. Religion, on the other hand, is a system of rules and traditions which, if kept by its followers, will supposedly cause them to gain acceptance with God. But religion can never bring man into a relationship with God.

When Paul says "the lying in wait of the Jews," he literally means the religious Jews who plotted against him, trying to tear down his reputation and his ministry, and even attempting to take his life. They were violently opposed to the doctrines of faith and grace Paul preached, looking to the law and Jewish tradition for salvation and truth.

Some of the biggest opposition a pastor faces will not be from the world or from the newspapers; it will be from the church down the street. But you must recall also that Jesus' biggest problem during His ministry on earth was the religious Jews, not the sinner on the street.

They can be from another denomination or of your same persuasion, but they're jealous because some of the members of their church left to go to yours. So they start to gossip about you and run you down, picking anything they can find that is wrong with you or your church. In essence, they feel like all the churches in town are competing.

One of the most destructive beliefs a pastor can have is that he has a monopoly on his city. If someone else starts a church in his town, somehow he feels that the new pastors should check with him first. After all, he believes, "I am the apostle to this city, and nobody comes here to start a church unless I approve them first!"

That's the first indication that you're headed downhill! God will lift the anointing right off of your church! He'll find somebody else who will walk in love toward the other churches – regardless of what they say or do. God's not concerned with maintaining ministries or building your reputation; He's in the business of saving people and stabilizing them in His Word.

I would like to mention here, however, that if God has called you to begin a work in a city, especially if it is a smaller town, I would advise you to let the other pastors in the city know. This is only proper; it is just good manners. If you begin your ministry to the town by showing respect for the leaders who are already there, you might avoid many problems later.

Here's another scenario I've seen, too: One pastor starts a church and plods away for years to get a few hundred members. Then another pastor starts a church across town, and the thing mushrooms!

What took the first pastor years to accomplish, the second pastor does in a matter of months, so the first pastor becomes jealous and begins to run down the second pastor and his church. In the end, the church members are the ones who are hurt.

In the city where I pastor, Tulsa, Oklahoma, churches are starting everywhere. We lose some of our members as God calls them to another church, but I tell them, "If God wants you there, then go!"

One of the greatest things to me is when people say, "Pastor Bob, there is a little church starting over here, just twenty or thirty members, and we went there last week, and God just told us we're supposed to be there and help them."

"Praise God!" I tell them, "We'll miss you, but go! If God called you there, you'd get stagnant if you stayed here!"

Then there are also the times when someone will come up after a service and say, "Pastor Bob, we've been across town at (whatever church), and today God spoke to us that this is where He wants us to be, so we'd like to become members of your church today." In these moments, I am reminded that "*the Lord* adds to the church daily such as should be saved" (Acts 2:47).

Pastors and churches should not feel threatened by each other. We're all branch offices working for the same Boss! And I'm thoroughly convinced that if your whole city got saved, every church in town would be packed out. We don't have to steal sheep; we can go out and turn goats into sheep any day!

Now I should mention here that there are times when one of your sheep will come to you and say that they are leaving, and you know that something is wrong. This is where you leave the ninety-nine and go after the one. You find out where the problem is and minister to them. These are the sheep that go astray from the flock, fall into a crevice, and you need to go and haul them out and bring them back to the flock.

However, sometimes a member of the congregation will say they're leaving, and you know it's not right, but when you go after them and minister to them, they just turn up their tail and keep going. In such cases, let them go! Once you've talked to them two or three times, if they're still mad at you, what are you going to do?

When this occurred at our church, I asked the Lord what I should do, and He gave me some great wisdom. He said, "The one you go after is the one who trips and falls, not the one who turns up their tail and just leaves. You've got better things to do than go after a sheep who will not turn. Kick the dust off your feet and go on with what I've called you to do."

Some pastors are running around town, trying to soothe people's feelings and bring understanding, and if you do not use wisdom regarding this, it can become a waste of time. Life is too short to chase people who are hot, mad, or upset after you've done all you can. Leave them in the Lord's hands and forget it.

Again, it comes down to this: Do what God has called you and your church to do, regardless of what the church or pastor down the street says, and regardless of what Brother and Sister So-and-So say as they head out the door.

Pray for the churches in your town to prosper in the things of God, and walk in love toward them and their pastors. Most importantly, do not defend yourself, just keep teaching the Word of God, obeying the Holy Spirit, and let God defend you. Remember, "When a man's ways please the Lord, he maketh even his enemies to be at peace with him" (Proverbs 16:7).

## Don't Furl the Sails

In verse 20, Paul goes on to say, "And how I *kept back nothing* that was profitable unto you, but have shewed you, and have taught you publicly, and from house to house." Here, Paul uses a very picturesque Greek word for "kept back nothing," *hupostello.*

The word *hupostello* paints a picture of a sailing vessel on which none of the sails are "furled" or tied back. If you like to sail or know anything about sailing, you know that if the wind is blowing strongly and you don't want to travel that fast, you "furl the sails," or you fold the sails back to where very little of the face of the sail is catching the wind.

But Paul wants this ship (the local church) to go full speed ahead, as fast as the wind will carry it. The captain of this ship (the pastor) is not to fold back or "furl" any of the sails to try to hinder or slow down the ship as it travels toward its destination.

Literally, Paul is saying, "Do not furl the sails in the ministry. Whatever God has given you, whatever the Chief

16

Shepherd has fed you, you feed that to the sheep – hold nothing back."

Sometimes when ministers preach or teach to other ministers, they might be tempted to withhold some of the revelation God has given them in order to "corner the market" on a particular subject or issue. But Paul is commanding these pastors to share everything with their elders, bishops, and deacons, as well as their congregations.

Also, while you're ministering the Word of God to the people, many things come to you by the Holy Spirit. Sometimes revelation will come to me when I'm in the pulpit that I didn't study as I prepared the message. Verses of scripture will rise up that I hadn't thought of using before, or I might feel led of the Spirit to go off on a so-called "rabbit trail" for a few minutes.

But these things tie right in with what I'm saying, and there might be one person or a part of the congregation who needs to hear them. The Holy Spirit may even have me take a big detour just to set somebody free in a certain area.

Now let me make one distinction here. Paul is talking to pastors and elders of the local churches, who function very differently from someone who stands in the five-fold ministry office of the prophet (Ephesians 4:11).

There are times when a prophet of God may be restrained by the Holy Spirit from telling the people everything that has been revealed to him, simply because it is not the right time to reveal it. I have heard some genuine, proven prophets say, "God showed me this fifteen years ago, and He says the time has come to let you know," and it was exactly what the people needed at that time.

However, a pastor cannot do that. He cannot "furl the sails" or hold anything back from the people. When God shows something to him from the Word, he must give his congregation everything he has. *He cannot withhold grass from the sheep!*

# The Proof of Ministry

"And how I kept back nothing that was profitable unto you, but *have shewed you*, and have taught you publicly, and from house to house."

When he first came to Ephesus, Paul not only taught in the synagogue, he taught publicly in the School of Tyrannus, and in various homes of the people (see Acts 19:1-10). And when he says that he *showed* them the gospel along with teaching it, that means he lived it before them.

Paul trained these pastors. Many of them were his apprentices, some of them traveled with him, and many of them took churches that Paul had begun as an apostle. They were right there at his side when he preached the gospel and they saw many saved, miraculously healed, and set free.

The words "shewed you" and "taught you" are very important here, because ministry is not all preaching and teaching. Ministry is also "signs and wonders following" (Mark 16:20). The gospel is not only preached, it is demonstrated:

And these signs shall follow them that believe; In my name shall they cast out devils; they shall speak with new tongues;

They shall take up serpents; and if they drink any deadly thing, it shall not hurt them; they shall lay hands on the sick, and they shall recover.

So then after the Lord had spoken unto them, he was received up into heaven, and sat on the right hand of God.

And they went forth, and preached every where, the Lord working with them, and confirming the word with signs following.

Mark 16:17-20

Some people are born again when they hear the gospel preached; they hear the Word of God and receive it. Others are saved when they see a great miracle or healing, which is a sign and a wonder. Signs and wonders cause the fear of God to fall on people and receive Jesus as Lord and Savior.

For I will not dare to speak of any of those things which
Christ hath not wrought by me, to make the Gentiles
(heathen) obedient, by word and deed,

Through mighty signs and wonders, by the power of the
Spirit of God; so that from Jerusalem, and round about
unto Illyricum, I have fully preached the gospel of Christ.

Romans 15:18,19

You may be asking, "What does it mean 'to make the
Gentiles *obedient*'"? The Gentiles (unbelievers) become "obedient" (believers) when they receive Jesus as their Lord. They
were formerly in rebellion with Satan, but now they are in obe-
dience to God through Jesus Christ.

And how are they made obedient? The scripture goes on
to say how: "By *word and deed!*" In other words, the Gentiles
become obedient (receive salvation) by the preaching of the
Word of God, with signs and wonders following.

When Paul says "Word and deed," he is stressing the fact
that both God's Word and the power of the Holy Spirit are
involved in the preaching of the gospel. God's Word and power
must always be in balance in our lives. We never dismiss one
for the other, and where we have one, we should have the other.

There have been times in history when not one word was
spoken, but the sovereign hand of God was in demonstration
to the point that people would fall on their faces and accept
Jesus as their Savior. However, these new believers then
needed the "milk of the word that they may grow thereby"
(First Peter 2:2). So even in these unusual moves of God, the
Spirit and the Word will *both* be present.

"Through mighty signs and wonders, by the power of the
Spirit of God; so that from Jerusalem, and round about unto
Illyricum, I have fully preached the gospel of Christ."
According to this verse, you have not fully preached the gospel
until signs and wonders follow your ministry.

You can preach for hours, one sermon after another, and
pat yourself on the back – but there must be more than this!
Let God be God! Preach His Word, and then when your

19

preaching comes to an end, stand back and allow His power to break forth!

Then you will begin to understand that it's not by your eloquence or your great knowledge or abilities that people are saved and healed and delivered, but by the Spirit of God. As Paul said,

> **And my speech and my preaching was not with enticing words of man's wisdom, but in demonstration of the Spirit and of power:**
>
> **That your faith should not stand in the wisdom of men, but in the power of God.**
>
> **First Corinthians 2:4,5**

## House to House

Paul taught openly in fields, on the streets, and from house to house. In those times, many churches met in houses. Many of these pastors and elders were saved in the field or on the streets, but then as believers, they would fellowship together in houses. They grew up under Paul's ministry as he pastored them "from house to house."

In light of this, Paul tells them, "Remember my example. Don't furl the sails, preach the Word with power, and wherever the Holy Spirit leads, hold nothing back!"

## Chapter Three
# Bound in the Spirit

Testifying both to the Jews, and also to the Greeks, repentance toward our Lord Jesus Christ.

And now, behold, I go bound in the spirit unto Jerusalem, not knowing the things that shall befall me there:

Save that the Holy Ghost witnesseth in every city, saying that bonds and afflictions abide me.

But none of these things move me, neither count I my life dear unto myself, so that I might finish my course with joy, and the ministry, which I have received of the Lord Jesus, to testify the gospel of the grace of God.

Acts 20:21-24

IN THE FIRST VERSE OF THIS PASSAGE of scripture, verse 21, Paul says that he testified both "to the Jews and to the Greeks." Now why is this important for these pastors to hear? Because the gospel is for everyone, and Paul is reminding them of that fact. God has never excluded anyone from being saved because of race, color, nationality, how they dressed, or wore their hair!

Romans 1:16 says that the gospel is "the power of God unto salvation to *every one* that believeth; to the Jew first, and also to the Greek." Remember that the gospel was preached first to the Jew, then to the Gentile. The gospel is all-inclusive.

In the Old Testament, we see where God gave the plan of salvation to the nation of Israel through the law and the sacrifices. Then it was their responsibility to take it to all the nations of the world. An example of this is when God told Jonah to go to Nineveh (a Gentile city) and preach.

There are great examples of Gentile revivals in the Old Testament. Some of these Gentile believers, such as Ruth and Rahab the Harlot, were even added to the genealogical line that brought forth Jesus Christ (Matthew 1 and Luke 3).

But Israel failed to carry out God's will. By the time Jesus came on the scene, the Jews had become so entrenched in the religious rites and rituals now known as Judaism, consumed with the letter of the law instead of the Spirit of the law, that they did not recognize their own Messiah, Jesus of Nazareth.

This is why Jesus said to them in Matthew 21:43, "Therefore say I unto you, The kingdom of God shall be taken from you, and given to a nation bringing forth the fruits thereof."

In this verse, He was correctly prophesying that the gospel was being preached first to the Jew, but the Jewish nation would ultimately reject Him as their Messiah. Thus God would raise up a spiritual nation primarily of Gentiles, who would take the gospel to the world. He was prophesying about the Church Age.

## Paul's Calling

When Paul says, "Testifying both to the Jews, and also to the Greeks," he is referring to the fact that he himself has preached and taught in synagogues to the Jew and on the streets to the Gentile, just as Jesus did. However, the Book of Acts makes it clear that Paul was called *first* to the Gentiles.

Jesus revealed Paul's calling in Acts 9:15 when He said to Ananias, "Go thy way: for he (Paul) is a chosen vessel unto me, to bear my name before the Gentiles, and kings, and the children of Israel."

Notice that Paul is to bear the name of Jesus first to the Gentiles, then before kings, and lastly to the Jew. But in Acts 20:21, Paul reverses the order! He mentions first that he testified to the Jew, and then to the Gentile (Greek).

You will see why this is important in verse 22. This is one indication that Paul's priorities are out of order, that he is about to step out of God's will.

## Paul's Passion

In Acts 20:22, Paul begins to tell the pastors of Ephesus that he plans to go to Jerusalem, despite a check in his spirit and repeated warnings from the Holy Spirit. He says, "And now, behold, I go *bound in the spirit* unto Jerusalem..."

Paul's spirit (notice that spirit is a small "s") is telling him not to go to Jerusalem, but in the next verses he is going to rationalize the "no" he senses in his spirit, into a "yes." Have you ever done that? God is telling you one thing, and you just rationalize it into something else. Your desires try to reshape God's will.

Remember that Paul's calling was *first* to the Gentiles (Acts 9:15, Galatians 2:7), but in Acts 20:21, he mentions his testimony "to the Jew first, and also to the Greeks." Paul is working against his calling because of his personal desire to see the church at Jerusalem (which is made up of Jewish believers) get back to the grace of God and out of the legalistic bondage into which they had slipped.

Another thing I want you to notice is that suddenly Paul is in a big hurry: "For Paul had determined to sail by Ephesus, because he would not spend the time in Asia: for *he hasted*, if it were possible for him, to be at Jerusalem the day of Pentecost" (Acts 20:16).

One of the ways you know you could be missing God's will is when you're being pressured by time. Very often, the devil is the one who says that you'd better do something right now or you're going to be out of God's will. The Holy Spirit doesn't tell you to do something new or major the day before it is due! He gives you enough time to question Him and wait on Him to confirm it, so you can be sure it's God's will.

From the verses of scripture that tell about Paul's decision to go to Jerusalem, it seems clear that the Holy Spirit is doing all He can do to get through to Paul: "...not knowing the things that shall befall me there: Save *that the Holy Ghost witnesseth in every city, saying that bonds and afflictions abide me."*

From the moment Paul made up his mind to go to Jerusalem, wherever he went someone would walk up to him and say, "Hey, you are not supposed to go to Jerusalem. You are going to be bound and thrown into prison."

I can just imagine that as he went from city to city and town to town, people would stop him and say, "Are you born again? Are you the guy I'm supposed to talk to? The Holy Spirit told me I am supposed to tell you not to go to Jerusalem."

This is one example the Bible gives about how the Holy Spirit will speak to you through other believers. It's usually a person who doesn't know anything about you. They come up to you and tell you exactly what you already know in your heart. In other words, the Holy Spirit will use an outside source to confirm what He's already shown you inwardly.

So first of all, Paul knows in his own spirit – he's "bound in his spirit" – that he is not to go to Jerusalem. Then, in the next verse, he says that everywhere he goes, the Holy Spirit has been using other believers to tell him the same thing.

However, in verse 24 Paul says, "But none of these things move me...." What is he saying? He is still going to do what he wants to do. He is determined, and we're going to find out just how determined he is in the rest of the verse: "neither count I my life dear unto myself, so that I might finish my course with joy, and the ministry, which I have received of the Lord Jesus, to testify the gospel of the grace of God."

Now everything Paul is saying sounds good, but his attitude is wrong and he's going to the wrong place. He is noble, but stupid! You know, you can have the right messages, you can preach and teach the Word of God, but nothing will be accomplished by your efforts if you're out of God's will.

I've had pastors tell me, "I've been at this church so long and nothing has worked out. I've preached and taught the Word, and when I study and prepare the anointing is so strong. But when I get up in the pulpit – nothing happens. I'm doing and saying all the right things and I'm miserable!"

Then I ask them a very basic question, "Are you in God's will? Are you sure you're supposed to pastor, and if so, are you supposed to be here?" In most cases, the answer is "no" to one of these questions, or they're just not really sure.

When Paul says, "I don't even count my life dear unto myself, even if I have to die while I'm there," it sounds very commendable! But why die out of God's will? Why give your life when you don't have to?

Paul has taken what the Holy Spirit and his spirit are saying, that afflictions and imprisonment await him if he goes to Jerusalem, and he has turned a type of self-imposed persecution into the will of God.

How often have you heard somebody say, "Well, if I am being persecuted, it must be the will of God"? But you can be persecuted because you are out of God's will, too! Peter tells us that it is fine to accept buffeting when you're *in* the will of God, but what glory is there when you are persecuted for your faults (First Peter 2:20)?

The Holy Spirit has not only witnessed to Paul in every city, but in the next chapter of Acts, chapter 21, he is going to be stopped on four specific occasions by people telling him not to go to Jerusalem. A prophet of God, Agabus, is going to tell him not to go. Even his own team members are going to tell him not to go (Acts 21:1-12).

Nevertheless, he is still going "to testify the gospel of the grace of God." Again, there couldn't be anything better than to walk into a legalistic place like Jerusalem and preach grace to them – sounds great, doesn't it? So why is the Holy Spirit trying to stop him?

The Holy Spirit knows that Paul could go there and preach grace under the greatest anointing and no one would accept him or the message. More than that, He knows that when he does try to preach grace to them, they are going to try to kill him! In other words, the Holy Spirit knows that the Jewish believers in Jerusalem have hardened their hearts by choosing to live by the law instead of the Spirit. He knows that it's not only a waste of time for Paul to go there, but it's dangerous as well.

Later, when Paul arrives in Jerusalem, the elders won't allow him to preach until he takes a legalistic vow (Acts 21:22-24). So Paul agrees to take an old religious, traditional vow – shave his head and fast for seven days – *so he can preach grace!* That's like saying, "Shall we continue in sin that grace may abound!" God forbid! (See Romans 6:1,2.)

Do you see that Paul has compromised the message of grace in order to preach it? He's now thinking that the end justifies the means. He is talking about preaching grace in Jerusalem, but he doesn't practice grace when he gets there.

When someone compromises the Word of God as a means to an end, they will lose what they have compromised to keep. In fact, before Paul's seven-day "cleansing" is over, the Jews are trying to kill him. He never gets to preach grace to them at all, and if the Roman soldiers had not stepped in, he would have been killed.

## Passion Versus Calling

One of the traps that I see the devil set for ministers is illustrated here in Acts, chapters 20 and 21. Here, Paul made the decision to go to Jerusalem, and then traveled there to minister to the Jews. He did this instead of continuing with the work God called him to, which was to minister the gospel to the Gentiles.

Everybody has their passions – issues that really get their blood boiling. With Paul, it was his own people, the Jews. In Romans, chapter 9, verses 3, he says, "For I could wish that myself were accursed from Christ for my brethren, my kinsmen according to the flesh."

Paul is so passionate about the Jews coming to Christ, that he says that if it were possible, he would give up his own salvation for theirs. And, with the situation in the Jerusalem church, the strong emotions he has for his people are joined by the passion he has for the doctrine he preaches so strongly: the grace of God.

Paul had been in Jerusalem some five years before and was probably appalled at the apostasy that was there among the

Jewish believers. Legalism had so crept into the church that they weren't even preaching the gospel, but the law.

The elders were preaching circumcision for salvation, and teaching Old Testament rules and regulations for the Christian life. It grieved Paul's heart that the law was being taught as the means of spirituality instead of God's grace.

Up to the time of the pastors' conference in Miletus, the Holy Spirit had used Paul twice to go to Jerusalem and re-establish the gospel of grace among the Jewish believers there. But each time Paul left, the legalistic Jews began to preach the law and preach the law, until the church slipped back into legalism worse than before.

Now, when the Holy Spirit is directing him to call a meeting of the pastors of Ephesus, Paul is once again overcome with his passion for his Jewish brethren in Jerusalem, who have fallen into spiritual bondage to the law once more. So he willfully disobeys the direction of the Holy Spirit, and steps out of God's will, allowing his feelings about a serious issue to interfere with what God has called him to do.

Because he avoids the Lord's warning, when he gets to Jerusalem, his own actions cut him off from all of God's protection and divine keeping power. He is almost beaten to death by the Jews, without uttering one word of the gospel. It is only because the Roman law and government step in that his life is spared.

All of us have to carefully guard our hearts and make certain that the works we are doing are really what we are called to do and not something that moves us emotionally. Remember that Satan will try to use our *passions* to distract and deceive us away from our *calling*.

There are many important issues and areas of need that the Body of Christ should be involved in, but that's why we are a Body and not just one member. Find out what area(s) God has called you to and give it all you've got.

This is true for churches as well as individuals. Some churches have a vision for teaching, others are led to concentrate on missions, while others are called to evangelize their city. Churches are as different and unique as the pastors who lead them.

If you, as a congregational member, have strong feelings about a certain area of ministry, feel free to mention it to the pastor. But do not become upset if he does not share your enthusiasm. Just like Paul, you may have a consuming passion for something, but it may not be God's will for the church you attend.

Members of my congregation are involved in and, in many cases, consumed with various important issues such as abortion, pornography, homosexuality, child abuse, and the homeless. As a pastor, I could let these areas overwhelm me and get myself and the church caught up in something which was not God's will. I, too, could be noble, but stupid!

That's why it is so important for the pastor to stay in prayer and continuous study of the Word, so that he can be sure what God's vision for his church is and stick to it. Second Peter, chapter one, says that through study of the Word of God, you "give diligence to make your calling and election sure" (verse 10).

If you have strong feelings about something, pray and ask God if this is something in which He wants you or your church to become actively involved. Check yourself and make certain you are getting enough time in the Word to maintain balance.

If it becomes clear that it is not God's will for you or your church to become involved, continue interceding for those who are called to be there. In this way, you can avoid wasting time, or even falling into destructive situations, by getting out of God's will.

## Ministers Make Mistakes

I think it's great that the Holy Spirit lets us see when a great man of God like Paul erred. It lets us all understand that ministers are human. They make mistakes, they sin, and they prove themselves to be human just like everybody else.

I constantly tell my congregation: I have a gift to teach the Word, but not to live it. I have to walk it out minute by minute, hour by hour, and day by day just like they do.

What's great about seeing Paul's fall here in the book of Acts is that we see how God still managed to stand him before kings (Agrippa and Caesar) and to go on to minister to the Gentile nations later. In other words, even when you sin, if you repent, God still has a plan for your life.

Now listen very carefully. When you go against God's will, it will always cost you something! In this case, Paul's actions cost him several years. So don't think I'm saying that it's acceptable to "sin now and repent later"!

What I am saying is, "My little children, these things write I unto you, that you sin not. And if any man sin, we have an advocate with the Father, Jesus Christ the righteous" (First John 2:1). And "If we confess our sins, he is faithful and just to forgive us our sins, and to cleanse us from all unrighteousness" (First John 1:9).

As I travel across the country, I see so many ministers who are not in the ministry today because they fell and could not bring themselves to go back to what God called them to do. This is a great tragedy.

There are cities and towns crying out for pastors and teachers who are driving taxicabs or waiting tables in total defeat. If that's you, then I encourage you to follow the Apostle Paul's example. As you repent, pick yourself up, dust yourself off, and get before God.

I have a test for you to see if God is through with your life: Put your hand over your heart, and if it is still beating, God is not finished with you! So go out and do what He tells you to do. The Body of Christ needs you and your gift, and you need to be where God has called you to be!

# Chapter Four
# Pure from the Blood of All Men

And now, behold, I know that ye all, among whom I have gone preaching the kingdom of God, shall see my face no more.

Wherefore I take you to record this day, that I am pure from the blood of all men.

For I have not shunned to declare unto you all the counsel of God.

Take heed therefore unto yourselves, and to all the flock, over the which the Holy Ghost hath made you overseers, to feed the church of God, which he has purchased with his own blood.

Acts 20:25-28

AS WE BEGIN IN VERSE 25, Paul is telling the pastors that they will not see him again, which causes them all tremendous grief. In verses 37 and 38, it says they all wept when he said this.

Their love for him as a spiritual father is probably greater than their love for their natural fathers (First Corinthians 4:15), because in the three years Paul was in Ephesus, they were saved and grew up spiritually under his leadership.

As we discussed earlier, Paul was the apostle who began the first church at Ephesus, and out of that great church came other churches. These pastors were raised up along with them under Paul's ministry. So they are very emotional when Paul announces that they will "see his face no more."

What they do not know is that they will see Paul's face again. After he is delivered out of prison, he will get to come by and see them one more time. But none of them knows this at this time, and in this verse of scripture, Paul believes he will never see them again.

## Practical Wisdom

In the previous verses of scripture, we saw that Paul was avoiding the leading of the Holy Spirit in his own life by deter-mining to go to Jerusalem. Nevertheless, what he is about to say to these pastors contains some of the greatest practical wisdom for ministers found in all of the New Testament.

Verse 25 goes on to say, "Wherefore I take you to record this day, that I am pure from the blood of all men." You may ask, "What does the word 'blood' mean here?"

In Leviticus 17:11, the Bible tells us that "the life of the flesh is in the blood...." This means that the very life of a human being is found in his or her blood. Therefore, blood represents the life of a person. So Paul is saying that he is pure (free) from the responsibility of the lives of all men.

How would you like to go to sleep at night knowing that you are free from the responsibility of your people? Paul is going to tell you how in the next verse, "For I have not shunned to declare unto you all the counsel of God."

The word "shunned" is *hupostello*, the same word we found in Acts 20:20 for "kept back." Paul is saying, "I have kept back nothing from you. I have not 'furled the sails' (see Chapter Two) when I came to declare all the counsel of God to you."

When you present everything God has given to you from His Word, when you hold nothing back, then you are free from the responsibility of your congregation's lives. After you have delivered the Word of God to the people, then the responsibil-ity to live for the Lord is theirs.

Let's look at Second Corinthians 6:11-13: "O ye Corinthians, our mouth is open unto you, our heart is enlarged." Now that doesn't mean that Paul had an enlarged heart physically, but spiritually. His heart was filled to capacity and overflowing with the Word of God.

Have you ever been so full of God's Word that you felt bigger in your spirit than in your body? Smith Wigglesworth, a powerful British evangelist whom God used mightily in the first half of the twentieth century, made the statement, "I am actually bigger on the inside than I am on the outside." That's what Paul is talking about here when he says, "...our heart is enlarged."

When he says, "...our mouth is open to you," it is because out of the abundance of the heart the mouth speaks. In other words, "I am not furling the sails with you. Whatever is in my heart, my mouth is speaking to you."

Then he goes on to say in the next verse, "You are not straitened in us, you are straitened in your own bowels." A better translation for this would be, "You are not hindered by us, but you are hindered by your own emotions." What a powerful statement!

Do you know what is wrong with most congregations today? They are emotionally crippled. They are dictated to by their emotions and their lives revolve totally around how they feel at the moment.

They will praise God if they *feel* like it, they will study the Bible if they *feel* like it, they will accept the sermon if they *feel* like it. Then they will talk about the pastor or anybody else in the congregation if they don't *feel* like they're doing a good job. They go by their feelings.

That's the way the Corinthians were, and Paul is saying to them, "You are not hindered by me. I am not your problem. Your emotions are your problem." Then, in the next verse, he tells them the cure for their problem: "be ye also enlarged."

In other words, "Stop focusing on how you feel, concentrate on the Word of God, and fill your heart to overflowing with God's Word." You know that you are starting to grow in the kingdom of God when you make the decision to live according to God's Word, instead of what you feel from moment to moment.

You don't feel like praising God? Say to yourself, "Tough! I'm going to praise and worship the Father in spirit and in truth" (John 4:23)! You are no longer hindered by your emotions; you are letting your heart, which is filled with the Word of God, dictate your actions.

The mark of a mature believer is taking full responsibility for living out the Word of God in his or her life. When they make a mistake or fail somewhere, their first question is, "God, where did I miss it?"

But the immature believer will flounder and make mistakes, and then blame the church or someone else. It's the pastor's fault for not preaching right, or the congregation hasn't been supportive enough.

That's why Paul is saying to this carnal, immature body of believers in Corinth, "It's not my fault if you are not growing up spiritually. You are not hindered by me. Why? Because I poured out to you the Word of God that is within me. Now, the responsibility for your lives is in your hands."

## The Whole Counsel of God

One of the major reasons Paul could boldly declare that he was "pure from the blood of all men" is found in Acts 20:27: "For I have not shunned to declare unto you *all the counsel of God.*" "All the counsel of God," or the whole counsel of God, means every area of doctrine found in the Bible.

Some ministers "ride a hobby horse" – they only minister on one or two areas in the Word of God which are their favorites. But Paul is telling the pastors of Ephesus that they must teach the whole counsel of God, every area of the Word of God, in order to fulfill their responsibility as a minister to the people.

When a pastor teaches only a few doctrines and ignores the rest of the Scripture, not only will it produce an imbalanced congregation, but their "blood" will be on his head. For example, if a pastor refuses to preach the new birth (John 3:3, Romans 10:9,10), and therefore none of his people receive salvation, God will hold that pastor accountable.

As a pastor, you need to deliver the whole of the Word of God, not just the parts you like, in both the Old and New Testaments. Paul commended the pastor at Colosse (Epaphras), who prayed that his congregation "might stand perfect and complete in *all* the will of God" (Colossians 4:12). You can only pray for your people to stand in all the will of God if you are preaching and teaching all the will of God, which is His Word to them.

Many ministers shy away from preaching certain areas of the Word of God because those areas have been taken to an extreme by other ministers. Pastors may have seen believers get hurt because they followed after a ministry that took a certain doctrine and twisted it, so they stay away from the issue altogether.

Sometimes ministers stay away from doctrines that are controversial or deal with very private issues in our lives; at other times, they just avoid areas of the Word of God because they seem boring.

Jesus compared the Word of God with "our daily bread," or the food we eat every day to maintain our health and get the energy we need to be productive. Like the food in our natural lives, the Bible contains all different kinds of spiritual food, from fried chicken to ice cream to broccoli!

When we eat food in the natural, we must eat a balanced diet to be healthy. When we go to school, they teach us about the basic food groups, and that we need to eat all kinds of foods every day in order to feel good. We learn that if we eat nothing but candy every day, we cannot stay healthy.

The same principle holds true for spiritual food. In order for a congregation to grow and remain strong, the people need "all the counsel of God." Yes, there may be some complaining when you put liver and onions out from time to time, and some people may be unwilling to leave the apple pie and go on to try the Brussels sprouts! But in the end, you will have a healthier, stronger congregation if you explain the importance of and then give them "all the counsel of God" (Second Timothy 3:16,17)

The pastor who truly loves his congregation and wants to see them excel in every area of their lives will preach and teach everything the Bible has to say. When it comes to the controversial issues or those areas that have been taken to extremes, he will study them out for himself and teach his people what the Word of God actually says.

When it comes to the more intimate areas, he will tackle these subjects with confidence and boldness, trusting God to give him wisdom in presenting the truth in just the right way.

And when it's time to teach the areas of God's Word that seem less than exciting, he will pray for the eyes of his and their understanding to be enlightened to the richness and power in these important doctrines and principles. Usually, when a pastor is excited about what he's teaching, his excitement will be contagious, and his congregation will become excited, too!

In the day in which we're living, believers need to know what the Word of God says. With so much deception and so many opinions and philosophies in the world today, subtly bombarding our minds through television, movies, and publications, we need to know what *God* says.

That's why the Holy Spirit takes us to task in Hebrews 5:12-14 when He says:

> **For when for the time ye ought to be teachers, ye have need that one teach you again which be the first principles of the oracles of God; and are become such as have need of milk, and not of strong meat.**

> **For every one that useth milk is unskilful in the word of righteousness: for he is a babe.**

> **But strong meat belongeth to them that are of full age, even those who by reason of use have their senses exercised to discern both good and evil.**

If you are a pastor or are getting ready to step out into full-time ministry, you better not still be wanting a bottle! You had better have grown in the Word and in your relationship with God to the place where you are eating meat and not just drinking milk, where even your senses can "discern both good and evil."

You see, the Bible says that the Word of God is a "discerner of the thoughts and intents of the heart. Neither is there any creature that is not manifest in his sight: but all things are naked and opened unto the eyes of him with whom we have to do (Jesus)" (Hebrews 4:12,13). In other words, when you are strong in the Word and are walking with the Lord, very little will escape you!

If a deceiver comes along, you will discern him immediately. If a false doctrine is taught, the Word in you will expose it and eliminate it. God wants us all to rise to "full age," to build a solid foundation from which we can effectively reach this generation with the gospel and be a light in this dark world. But in order for this to happen, our churches must be well-fed on a balanced diet, which means "the whole counsel of God."

## Feed the Flock

Again, Paul says in Acts 20:26,27, "Wherefore I take you to record this day, that I am pure from the blood of all men. For I have not shunned to declare unto you all the counsel of God."

He goes on to say, "Take heed therefore unto yourselves, and to all the flock, over the which the Holy Ghost hath made you overseers, to feed the church of God, which he hath purchased with his own blood."

For right now, we're going to skip over "Take heed therefore unto yourselves," because I want to deal with this subject more thoroughly in the next chapter. We're going to go right on with "Take heed…to all the flock, over the which the Holy Ghost hath made you overseers, to feed the church of God…."

The Greek word for "made" is *tithemi*, which means "to place or appoint," and the word "overseers" is *episkopos*, which means "overseer or bishop." This verse of scripture says that the Holy Ghost appoints the pastor to oversee the flock, and that means that He gives the pastor the vision for that particular local church.

Verse 28 continues with, "...to feed the church of God...." The Greek word for "feed" is *poimen*, which means "pastor or shepherd," a clear reference to preaching and teaching the Word of God to the people.

This verse of scripture gives the two areas of responsibility for the pastor: 1) preaching and teaching the Word of God (feed); and 2) receiving and carrying out the vision for the church (lead).

God has called me to pastor, which means that a major portion of my time is spent studying God's Word, and as I do to stay before Him in prayer to get direction for the church over which He has made me overseer.

It's interesting to note that in Ephesians 4:11, there is no break between pastor and teacher in the original Greek. Literally, most scholars agree that "pastor" is a title and "teacher" is the function of the pastor. I stand in the office of a pastor, and my job is to teach. Therefore, I'm a "pastor-teacher." While it is true that you can stand in the office of a teacher without being a pastor (First Corinthians 12:28), *you cannot be a pastor without being a teacher.*

Some people think that the pastor is primarily a counselor. While it's right for a pastor to do some counseling, that is not his major calling. His primary responsibility is to study God's Word and pray. Then he can lead the people in the will of God and feed them well with His Word.

God raises up congregational members to become deacons, elders, and bishops within the local church body. These men and women are called to assist the pastor by taking on the duties of counseling, visitation, music ministry, and the other functions of the church.

From time to time the pastor will counsel, visit, and if he is gifted in this way, he may even sing a song (I know one pastor who plays his guitar during praise and worship). However, his first priority is to the Word of God and prayer, and by delegating various ministry opportunities to others, he is able to succeed in study and prayer.

Someone came up to me once and said, "You've got to get out and visit everybody or the church will fall apart." I said,

"Well, I didn't visit them to get them to come in the first place." You see, they come because they enjoy the Word of God and being in God's presence during the services.

In Acts 6:7, it says that the number of disciples increased, and even many Jewish priests became believers, *as the Word of God was preached.* Why not stick with the plan we know is successful?

Now this doesn't excuse pastors from counseling or visiting anyone, but it means they must prayerfully seek the direction of the Holy Spirit to know when to do these other things. You must be selective in order to keep your priorities in line with God's Word.

Also, if the pastor did everything, no one else would get into the ministry! Where do you start when you know God has called you to full-time ministry? You don't start in the pulpit – you start by putting your hand to the plow in the local church. You visit the sick and pray for them, you sing in the choir, or become one of the counselors.

From these positions, God will promote you as you are faithful (First Timothy 3:13). There are great missionaries from our church who used to be our janitors or run our sound equipment, and there are gifted pastors across America who used to usher or work in our counseling department.

Again, God raises up all these people to free the pastor's time for study and prayer. When I counsel someone, I'm reaching only one person. But when I teach the Word from the pulpit, I'm doing my most effective job, because I'm reaching more people. My anointing is strongest when I'm in the pulpit doing the primary thing God called me to do: *feed the flock.*

## Supernatural Striving

Romans 15:20 says, "Yea, so have I strived to preach the gospel...." There is a striving to preach the gospel, and to study, pray, and teach the Word of God. The striving is against Satan and the flesh as you try to spend time before God.

Satan opposes the ministry more than anything else. I've had people tell me, "I never had this much opposition when I was driving a cab or working at the grocery store. I got into the ministry and it seemed like all hell broke loose!"

The Word of God tells us that Satan is the accuser of the brethren, and there are many examples in the Bible of him doing this to great spiritual leaders, such as Job (Job 1:9-11) and Joshua, the high priest (Zechariah 3:1-4). He brings the greatest pressure upon spiritual leadership because he knows that if he breaks the leader, he can destroy the followers.

Satan also knows that your time before God produces a knowledge of the Word coupled with a supernatural ministry. Signs and wonders follow those who spend time waiting on the Lord, and therefore he will try to prevent you from doing that. So you must strive to overcome his hindering tactics and persevere in the Word and prayer.

Even though there is a cost to a supernatural ministry, the rewards are tremendous. As you strive to maintain a ministry which operates in the power of the Holy Spirit, you will produce a ministry which causes the unbeliever to accept Jesus Christ, the lame to walk, and the blind to see. This does great damage to Satan's rule!

And there is a personal benefit to this striving. Second Peter 1:10 says, "Wherefore the rather, brethren, give diligence (to the Word of God) to make your calling and election sure: for if ye do these things, ye shall never fail." You will never doubt your salvation or your calling, and your life and ministry will become completely stable and dependable, as you are faithful to the Word and prayer.

Now you can't follow any one person's *method* for getting in the presence of God and seeing His power work in your life, but you can learn *principles* from others. I know one minister, a powerful minister of God, who prays in the Spirit many hours a day. His lifestyle encourages the rest of us to pray in the Spirit, but should not make us imitate his method.

I've met ministers who fast before services and others who eat. Some take a nap, walk alone, or are quiet before the Lord before they go to minister. They have spent a great deal of time developing their relationship with the Lord and striving to understand how the Holy Spirit wants to work through them.

Satan opposes these supernatural ministries because the results are so great. When many people have their needs met, many more will accept Jesus as their Lord and Savior. So the devil tries to prevent pastors from spending time studying the Word of God and communing with the Holy Spirit in prayer.

The moment you sit down to study and pray, every tactic will be used to stop you. You may have cut yourself off from the world by giving your secretary instructions that you are not to be disturbed except by an emergency, but you will still have to deal with the devil and your flesh.

Satan will see to it that you remember things you need to do around the house, people in the church who should be contacted, and areas of need will loom before your eyes. Things you hadn't thought about in months will spring up unexpectedly.

If these devices don't succeed in distracting you, your flesh will try to sabotage your efforts. It will try everything, from terrible fatigue to the temperature of the room, to try to keep you from concentrating on Bible study and prayer.

However, your striving and perseverance in study and prayer will produce a close relationship between you and God that builds the solid foundation of an effective, powerful ministry.

## Whose Flock Are They?

Earlier we saw that a pastor is "free from the blood of all men" when he "holds nothing back," when he preaches the "whole counsel of God." But we know that if someone has a need, and the pastor fails to yield to the Holy Spirit and give out all that God gives him, the Holy Spirit can lead someone else to minister to that person in the hall, the lobby, or the parking lot. *Our failures do not hinder God.*

And that leads us to the next point in this verse of scripture: "...to feed the church of God, *which he hath purchased with his own blood.*" I want you to notice that the ultimate responsibility for the flock is on the Lord Jesus Christ, because He purchased us with His blood, and the entire Church belongs to Him.

He is the Chief Shepherd, the Ultimate Pastor. If the undershepherd makes a mistake, if the pastor fails in some way, Jesus will see to it that the church members are ministered to by someone else.

You see, Pastor, you must remember that they are not *your* sheep! They are called the church *of God*. Your job is to lead them and feed them as the Holy Spirit directs, and then it is up to them to believe it and live it. I tell my congregation, "If I make a mistake, you still have a Chief Pastor Who never fails!"

The pastor didn't purchase the Church, God did. Therefore, God is the rightful owner of the Church of Jesus Christ. And He purchased the Church with the precious blood of His Son, so that makes all believers very precious to Him. The "sheep of His pasture," the members of the Body of Christ, are the most valuable possession God has.

What an awesome privilege it is when God gives a pastor the solemn responsibility to oversee and feed His most precious possession. You say, "How do you sleep at night?" I can sleep in peace only because I know that, first of all, they are not my sheep, they are not my people, and secondly, I am "pure from their blood," because I have kept nothing back from them that God has shown me.

God has asked me to find food for them and He has given me the place to get it. All He asks me to do is to prayerfully find it, prepare it, and put it out in front of the sheep. Then it's up to them to eat it and up to God to do the rest.

I can't heal anybody. I can't save anybody. I can't restore anybody's family. All I can do is pray and present the Word of God, expecting the Holy Spirit to draw them in and meet their needs. I just do my part and trust God to do His, praying for the sheep to receive it all. That's how I can sleep in peace – *"pure from the blood of all men"!*

# Chapter Five
# Take Heed to Yourselves

IN VERSE 28 OF ACTS, CHAPTER 20, Paul exhorts the pastors of Ephesus to "Take heed therefore unto yourselves, and to all the flock...." I want to ask you something – when it comes to the ministry, which comes first, you or your flock?

If you carefully examine the verse above, you will discover that the Word of God commands you to put yourself *before* your flock. This doesn't mean that you slight your congregation in any way, but you actually aid and assist your people when you take care of yourself and your family first. Obviously, the more healthy and balanced your *life* is, the more productive and effective your *ministry* will be.

In Philippians 2:4, Paul also says "Look not every man on his own things, but every man also on the things of others." A better translation would be, "Don't consider only your own interests, but also consider the interests of others." In other words, we are to set priorities.

From these verses of scripture, the precedent is established that God wants you to take care of yourself and set priorities in your life. Then you will be able to take care of the flock to the best of your ability and fulfill your calling with joy.

## Daily Schedules

I find in my own life that there is nothing predictable in the ministry. There are times when I would love to work for a fast-food place, where you just put the meat on the bun and go home. At five o'clock, you leave the meat and the buns, and forget about them until the next day.

But in the ministry anything can happen at any moment, and adjustments often need to be made in both work and private schedules. Also, if you are not diligent to remember that you are "pure from the blood of all men" (see Chapter Four), everything can go home with you. A great mental pressure can arise as you identify with the needs of the people and as you try to figure out how to meet all those needs.

That's why it's so important to have a schedule that's based on priorities, but flexible enough to take into account the unexpected. The Word of God says, "Where there is no vision, the people perish" (Proverbs 29:18), and *there needs to be a daily vision to go along with the long-range vision.*

Remember that most of the scriptures that deal with time talk about the day: "His mercies are new every morning" (Lamentations 3:22,23), "I may daily perform my vows " (Psalms 61:8), "Give us this day our daily bread" (Matthew 6:11), and "Exhort one another daily" (Hebrews 3:13).

## Spiritual Workaholic

Yet I supposed it necessary to send to you Epaphroditus, my brother, and companion in labour, and fellow-soldier, but your messenger, and he that ministered to my want.

For he longed after you all, and was full of heaviness, because that ye had heard that he had been sick.

For indeed he was sick nigh unto death: but God had mercy on him; and not on him only, but on me also, lest I should have sorrow upon sorrow.

I sent him therefore the more carefully, that, when ye see him again, ye may rejoice, and that I may be the less sorrowful.

Receive him therefore in the Lord with all gladness; and hold such in reputation:

Because for the work of Christ he was nigh unto death, not regarding his life, to supply your lack of service toward me.

**Philippians 2:25-30**

44

In these verses of scripture there is a rebuke toward ministers to not be spiritual workaholics. Epaphroditus nearly died because he worked and worked in the ministry and did not consider his own well-being.

The phrase "not regarding his life" literally means in the Greek that he is like a fighter who goes into the ring, knowing his opponent is much stronger and that he is totally out of shape. He knows that he's going to get beat up, which is exactly what happened to Epaphroditus.

What this passage is bringing out is that this man was weak, he was tired, and he was sick, but he didn't know when to quit. He put the needs of others so high above himself that he actually worked himself to the point of death.

Epaphroditus had such a distorted vision of the ministry that he never went to Paul to tell him, "Look Paul, I'm tired. I'm worn out and sick, and I need to take some time off." No, he just kept working and would have died except for Paul's prayer of intercession.

You might be thinking, "I'm glad Epaphroditus rose up in faith and God healed him." But that's not what happened! The reason God healed him was that He had mercy on *Paul* "lest *he* should have sorrow upon sorrow."

What does "sorrow upon sorrow" mean? Paul was already in prison, and he didn't want to lose his friend on top of that, so God healed Epaphroditus as an act of mercy toward Paul.

In other words, Paul is saying, "Epaphroditus wasn't healed because he believed God, he was spared on my account. He was acting foolishly and killing himself with work, and I begged for mercy – for him and for me – and God healed him."

## A Balanced Life

It is not God's will for you to work yourself into the ground for the ministry. I find that across the country ministers are discouraged, ready to give up, and just flat-out tired. We call it "burnout" and many other things, but this condition doesn't have to occur. It can be avoided by using practical wisdom from the Word of God.

I've heard ministers say, "Well, bless God, I would rather wear out for God than rust out for the devil." Wait a minute – why do either one? Why can't you live till ninety, one hundred, or one hundred and ten, and still keep preaching?

People who have a workaholic attitude usually put others under condemnation for not working as hard as they do. Then they either die early, or, what's worse, they get so burned out and tired that they quit the ministry and don't want anything to do with it.

But let's go back to the scripture in Philippians 2:4, "Look not every man on his own things, but every man also on the things of others." There is a time for yourself and a time to give to others.

I've noticed that some people seem to make a choice in the ministry. They either look only at their own needs or they look only at the needs of others. But we should have the mind of Christ. We should consider our own needs as well as the needs of others. There should be a balance.

Realize that the ministry is demanding, and even though it can be exciting, and the anointing is great, we are still treasures in earthen vessels. What good is it going to do you or your congregation if you drop dead at forty-five years old?

Now I realize some ministers get burned out because they take their eyes off the Lord, don't stay in the Word and prayer, etc. But I meet more ministers who just don't know when to rest. They will work all day, into the night, all week long.

Solomon said, "To every thing there is a season, and a time to every purpose under heaven" (Ecclesiastes 3:1). There is a time to work and there is a time for rest. The man of wisdom will listen to the needs of the flock, the needs of his family, and the needs of his own body. He will know when to take heed to each one.

Take heed unto thyself, and unto the doctrine; continue in
them: for in doing this thou shalt both save thyself, and
them that hear thee.

First Timothy 4:16

Paul exhorts Timothy to learn to take care of himself and
stay in the Word, then he will "save himself and his people."
Paul says, "Timothy, if you take good care of yourself, if you
live what you preach from the Word of God, not only will you
live a balanced, productive, and happy life, but you will be
doing your congregation a great favor, too!"

What's interesting is that "yourself" even comes before
the Word. I've always been strong on the Word, and I consider
it the highest priority in ministry. I shut myself off for hours
every day to study and meditate in the Bible.

Some ministers don't believe studying the Bible is that
important, however. They will drop it in a second to talk to
somebody on the phone or go see somebody. But I take Acts
6:4 literally, that full-time ministers "give ourselves continually (which means "primarily") to prayer, and to the ministry of
the word."

So I tell my secretary that during certain hours of the day
I cannot be disturbed, and I give myself to prayer and study,
prayer and study, prayer and study. Then the rest of my
working day can be filled with meetings with my staff, coun-
selling, or visitation.

Praying and studying the Word of God is one area where
I could easily overdose, though! I could study all day at the
office and neglect other things. Then I could go home and
study some more, which would deprive my family of the attention they need. A "studyholic" is as bad as a "workaholic" in
the ministry.

That's why Paul takes time to tell Timothy that it's possible to burn yourself out even in studying the Word! "Take
heed to yourself, and to the Word of God," or, "Remember to
give yourself some time off, even from the Word of God,
Timothy. You need to set aside some time for *total* relaxation."

# There's No Condemnation
# in Taking a Vacation!

Pastors don't mind if the members of their churches take a vacation, and First Peter 5:3 says the pastor is to be an example for the flock, so why are they so concerned about what the congregation will think if they take a vacation, too?

Let me ask you, do you think Paul would ask Timothy and Epaphroditus and the pastors of Ephesus to take heed to themselves and not do it himself? In fact, after his first missionary journey, the Bible says he took a lengthy sabbatical in Antioch (Acts 14:26-28). He had been gone for a long time, so he rested there for awhile. Then, after his second missionary journey to Ephesus, he rested again. Paul came to the pastors' conference in Miletus directly from a vacation. Let's look at Acts 20:14-15:

> And when he (Paul) met with us at Assos, we took him in, and came to Mitylene.
>
> And we sailed thence, and came the next day over against Chios; and the next day we arrived at Samos, and tarried at Trogyllium; and the next day we came to Miletus.

We know that no scripture is in the Bible by accident, that all scripture is given by inspiration of God and is profitable, so why in the world are these verses in here – he went to this place, he went to that place – places we may never have heard of before.

I'll tell you why: because all of these places are resort areas! They are some of the most fabulous, beautiful spots in the world, in the warmest parts of the Mediterranean area, with the best hotels, finest food, and whitest beaches. And Paul is going on a holiday, traveling from one resort to the next just to rest and relax!

Now I want you to know that, like our modern day resort areas, these islands and cities were filled with sin, and they were filled with people who needed to meet the Lord. All of these places had great spiritual need.

Take Mitylene, for example. It was the capitol city of the island of Lesbos, from which we get the English word for lesbian. Needless to say, it was one of the ancient world's great resort spots for lesbians.

The Bible says that Paul only stopped off the coast of Chios. This was one of the more popular places, due to its manufacture of the best wine in the ancient world. Rich people came to wine and dine here, and to enjoy the beautiful climate.

The island of Samos was where the ancient world worshipped Hairoh, a Greek goddess, in the same manner that the Ephesians worshipped Diana. Men would come into the temple with meat offerings and then have sex with the priestesses.

All of the places Paul stopped, though beautiful, had tremendous need for the gospel, but these scriptures do not say, "Paul went to Samos and preached," or "Many were saved at Chios." Why did he go to these places? To lie on the beach and get a tan!

Paul learned to take time off between times of ministry. But so many ministers today can't lie on the beach without letting the devil condemn them. I can see Paul lying there on the warm sand, covered with suntan lotion, and Luke turning to him and saying, "Paul, look at all these sinners. Don't you think we ought to go witness to them?"

I can just hear Paul say, "Not today, Luke. It's time to relax, rest, and just enjoy ourselves for awhile."

Understand something: there were times when Paul marched right into a group of people and preached, there were times when God supernaturally crossed his path with people who were ready to be saved, and then there were these times when he was not led to witness to anyone.

The same holds true in our own lives. *We are to be witnesses in this earth, but we are to be led by the Holy Spirit.* And there are times when He will not lead you to speak of the gospel, even in the midst of unbelievers who need to be saved.

I'm not saying that Paul never witnessed to anyone during his vacations, but the Word of God doesn't say that he did. Certainly, if the Holy Spirit leads you to minister to someone, no matter where you are or what you're doing, then minister. But if you're on vacation and you're not led to minister, enjoy yourself and relax! Again, as Ecclesiastes 3:1 says, there is a time for everything.

Also, remember that the Bible says there are those in the congregation "given to hospitality" (Romans 12:13). That says to us that hospitality is part of the Christian life! Hospitality is one of the things we find in Acts, chapter 2, that made the early church successful. The early church spent time eating and having fellowship with one another.

Whether you talk about the ministry or not, Christians ought to have the best fellowship in the world. In fact, their parties ought to put the world's to shame! I enjoy just being around other believers and having fun. It's refreshing and brings balance to my life.

I know some Christians who go to a party and try to turn it into a prayer meeting or a Bible study. They feel condemned if they have a good time, like they're sinning. But Paul laid on the beach in total peace, because he knew God could get somebody else to preach while he rested!

A mistake ministers often make is assuming they are the only one God can use in a particular situation or area. They minister because of the needs they see, instead of according to the leading of the Holy Spirit. Not even Jesus was led by the needs of the people. He was led by the Holy Spirit – and He went to parties (John 2:1,2) and took time off (Mark 6:31,32)!

I heard one minister say that he couldn't bear to leave his congregation, and after two or three years of preaching every service (he wouldn't even have a guest minister), he had a physical breakdown. While he was hospitalized, he was under such mental anguish that the church had to be turned over to the associate pastor, who hadn't preached very much because the pastor was always in the pulpit.

Later he told me, "That was the best thing that ever happened to me." When I asked him why, he said, "Because after being away for a month, I went back to find that the church was bigger than when I left, and I began to realize that I was not as important as I thought I was."

Some ministers think the Body of Christ rises and falls on their ministry, but here's a big shock: God got along fine before you came along, and He can get along fine after you are gone. Yes, you are important, unique, and special. And yes, you have your place in the Body of Christ. But one of the worst things you can do is to think of yourself more highly than you ought to think (Romans 12:3).

So take a vacation! Take time off! Go to clean Christian parties once in awhile! And trust God that while you're away He can work through the bishops and elders and deacons He's raised up in your church to help you carry out the vision He's given you.

I've told my congregation that I will take time off. I take two vacations a year, one in the summer and one in the winter. And then from time to time my wife and I just take off for a night or two and spend some time by ourselves. I also go to a pastors' conference from time to time.

God wants us to have time for spiritual refreshing, like pastor's conferences and seminars, but also for natural refreshing, like vacations. And it's just common sense that the more refreshed and healthy you are, the more you can give to your people when you return.

## Family Before Ministry

I don't get too many "amens" from ministers on this one, but the Bible says that your family comes before your ministry.

And whatsoever ye do in word or deed, do all in the name of the Lord Jesus, giving thanks to God and the Father by him.

Wives, submit yourselves unto your own husbands, as it is fit in the Lord.

Husbands, love your wives, and be not bitter against them.

Children, obey your parents in all things: for this is well pleasing unto the Lord.

51

**Fathers provoke not your children to anger, lest they be discouraged.**

**Servants, obey in all things your masters according to the flesh...**

Colossians 3:17-22

This passage of scripture sets priorities in our Christian lives: God comes first, then our husband or wife, then our children, then our profession. If your profession is full-time ministry, it comes after your relationship with God and your family. If you have a part-time ministry, it comes after your relationship with God, your spouse, your children and your paying profession.

What a sad thing to win souls for the kingdom of God and lose your wife and/or children. If your family is falling apart, no one would blame you for taking time off from your ministry to straighten things out.

This is so important: *God can get another pastor for your congregation, but you are the only husband to your wife, the only father your children have.*

How many times has the family become jealous of the ministry? If you tell your family that you are going to take a day off and it never happens, it causes them to be discouraged. And when you finally do take a vacation, you are so wrapped up in the ministry that you can't relax, have a good time, and be a part of their lives.

In the end, this seemingly dedicated minister runs himself into the ground and drives his family away from himself, the ministry, and the things of God.

Ministers like that used to make me feel guilty – but not anymore! I take time off away from the church and enjoy my family, thanking God for them and the great staff He's provided to run things while I'm away. I can do this because I realize that the church I pastor doesn't rise and fall on me; it sets squarely on the shoulders of Jesus Christ!

# Jethro's Advice

There is no more beautiful example of a pastor and a congregation than Moses and the nation of Israel. Can you imagine having a church of two to three million? That's what Moses had, and I want you to notice that there was just one Moses, just one head, even though he pastored a great multitude.

In Exodus 18, beginning with verse 13, the Bible says, "And it came to pass on the morrow, that Moses sat down to judge the people: and the people stood by Moses from the morning unto the evening." Obviously, the line outside Moses' door went from sand dune to sand dune, and he was putting the flock before himself.

"And when Moses' father in law saw all that he did to the people, he said, What is this thing that thou doest to the people? why sittest thou thyself alone, and all the people stand by thee from morning unto even?" Jethro, Moses' father-in-law, is getting ready to give his son-in-law some good godly counsel about delegating authority.

"And Moses said unto his father in law, Because the people come unto me to inquire of God: When they have a matter, they come unto me; and I judge between one and another, and I do make them know the statutes of God, and his laws." Moses is very impressed with his job, but it's killing him!

"And Moses' father in law said unto him, The thing that thou doest is not good. Thou wilt surely wear away, both thou, and this people that is with thee: for this thing is too heavy for thee; thou are not able to perform it thyself alone. Hearken now unto my voice, I will give thee counsel."

First, I think it's interesting that Jethro did not dictate to Moses; he said, "I'm going to give you a little advice." Also, he told Moses that not only was this whole operation not good, but it was going to eventually give him a physical breakdown. Then where would the people be?

"I will give thee counsel, and God shall be with thee: Be thou for the people to Godward, that thou mayest bring the causes unto God. And thou shalt teach them ordinances and laws...." Jethro tells Moses that his priorities are all wrong. His greatest ministry was to be an intercessor to God for the people's needs and to teach the Word to them. Moses needed to learn what Peter told the multitude in Acts 6:4, "We will give ourselves primarily to prayer and the ministry of the Word."

Jethro continues, "And thou shalt teach them ordinances and laws, and shalt shew them the way wherein they must walk, and the work that they must do. Moreover thou shalt provide out of all the people able men, such as fear God, men of truth (those that know the Word of God), hating covetousness; and place such over them, to be rulers of thousands, and rulers of hundreds, rulers of fifties, and rulers of tens."

The able men, who know the Word of God, fear Him, and are not looking for *position*, but to *serve*, are the elders and bishops and deacons that Moses will appoint. Again, we have one of the keys to a successful ministry: the principle of delegation.

I often get this question from pastors, "When do I start delegating authority?" Taking the scripture as our pattern, it is clear that you should begin delegating when you have ten people. Give someone else the responsibility to set up and put away the chairs. If you start delegating when you have ten, it will be much easier to delegate when you get to fifty.

Also, if you begin delegating when you have small numbers, by the time you have greater numbers you will know whom you can trust as elders and bishops over major areas in the church, because they will have had the opportunity to prove themselves faithful.

It has been my experience that the longer you wait to delegate, the more difficult it becomes to give up the various responsibilities of the church to others later on. Also, if you try to build the whole church yourself, when you attempt to release something to others, you will be tempted to keep such a tight rein on everybody, watching over them all the time, that you stifle their creativity and their ministry.

It's so important to learn to let go, to trust God to lead the ones to whom you've given responsibility. Then, the confidence you place in them as ministers will help encourage them to do the best job they can.

When you let go at ten, there's not as much at stake. So what if the chairs are not as straight as you placed them? Tell the guy to straighten them up, but don't go over and do it yourself! If you learn the principle of delegation at ten with setting up chairs, it's going to be a whole lot easier to turn over the counseling department when you have many more members.

"And let them judge the people at all seasons: and it shall be, that every great matter they shall bring unto thee, but every small matter they shall judge: so shall it be easier for thyself, and they shall bear the burden with thee."

Another pastor said something to me once that I have never forgotten. He said, *"God hasn't called you to minister to everybody. He has called you to see to it that everybody is ministered to."*

The staff of the church, whether paid or volunteer, should be able to eliminate ninety to ninety-five percent of the problems, and the other five or so percent can easily be handled by the pastor. And again, this allows the pastor to spend the time he needs in the Word and prayer.

"If thou shalt do this thing, and God command thee so, then thou shalt be able to endure, and all this people shall also go to their place in peace." Pastor, if you delegate, you and your congregation are going to live long, peaceful lives!

I would like to mention something here, too, about volunteers. If you are burning out as a volunteer, something is wrong. We try to rotate volunteers at our church, so that they have time with their families and can be fresh and enjoy their ministry here.

We also ask our volunteers to sign up to work for a certain length of time. For example, a children's worker agrees to participate for six months. When the six months comes to an end, they have the option of leaving or signing up for another period of time. In this way, both the volunteer and the paid staff know the extent of the volunteer's obligation to the church.

In some cases, I know that volunteers can get discouraged and have even left churches because the leadership of the church has taken advantage of their willingness to serve. The attitude is almost, "Bless God, we've got a volunteer! Let's wring everything out of them that we can!" This is something every pastor should try to avoid.

On the other hand, if you are a volunteer minister in the church, you should "Take heed therefore unto yourselves and to the Word of God!" Use good common sense and set priorities to live a balanced life, and then your volunteer work will not become a burden to you or your family.

One thing I use to monitor myself is this: Am I the same today as I was when I took the church? Do I spend as much time in the Word and prayer now as I did then? Are my priorities in line? Am I living a balanced life?

Do I spend as much time with my family as I did then? Am I delegating what needs to be delegated? Am I breaking away for times of spiritual refreshing and taking vacations for times of physical refreshing?

I want to be the same if the church grows to two million as I am now. What would I do if the church was two million? I'd have the biggest staff you ever saw! Because I don't want to drop dead of exhaustion at fifty or sixty. I would like to live to be one hundred twenty years old like Moses, preaching the Word of God and blessing the people!

These things are laid out in the Word of God so that we can live a long time on the earth and be as productive as possible. After all, Moses' eye was not dim at one hundred twenty years old, and Joshua conquered a mountain at the age of eighty-five.

I have told my congregation that I never plan to retire. I don't believe in working hard most of my life and then suddenly quitting. My prayer is to die in the pulpit in my old age, and my associate would just come up and finish the message as the ushers dragged my body out!

So the Word of God clearly states that the minister should put himself and his family before his ministry: *"Take heed therefore unto yourselves, and to all the flock...."*

# Chapter Six
# Watch and Remember

For I know this, that after my departing shall grievous wolves enter in among you, not sparing the flock.

Also of your own selves shall men arise, speaking perverse things, to draw away disciples after them.

Therefore watch, and remember, that by the space of three years I ceased not to warn every one night and day with tears.

Acts 20:29-31

PAUL BEGINS VERSE 29 with a confident declaration, "For I know this," – here's something the Holy Spirit has revealed to Paul – "that after my departing shall grievous wolves enter in among you, not sparing the flock."

Paul is warning the pastors of Ephesus that after his departure "grievous wolves" are going to come in. The word "grievous" here actually means "vicious and cruel." And notice that they "enter in," which means they are going to come *from the outside.*

Wolves are unbelievers that "enter in" to the local church from the outside. Later, in verse 30, Paul will discuss other false teachers and prophets who will rise up from the inside of the church. These are believers who, because of their pride, Satan uses to try to destroy the church *from the inside.* Remember, the enemy works to destroy the church both from without and within.

Therefore, in verse 31, Paul commands the pastors to *watch* for possible trouble, and *remember* that, externally or internally, the enemy is always working to try to break the power of what God is doing in the local church by causing confusion and disunity among the staff and the congregation.

# Wolves

The "grievous wolves who enter in among you" are unbelievers. Satan sends them into a church for the specific purpose of dividing and destroying that local body of believers (verse 29). Jesus called them "wolves in sheep's clothing" (Matthew 7:15).

Notice that Jesus said they come dressed in *sheep's* clothing, not *shepherd's* clothing. This means that they don't walk into the church and announce that they are the pastor. They try to infiltrate into the congregation, acting and sounding like one of the sheep, but secretly seeking to lead the sheep away from God's appointed shepherd and the faith.

The ones they usually carry away with them are the babies, the ones who are not knowledgeable about the basic doctrines of the Word of God. And remember, *wolves don't eat shepherds; they eat sheep.* They come in to capture the hearts and minds of unsuspecting and undiscerning church members, to draw them away, causing division and church splits.

Of course, the wolf behind all wolves is the one who "enters in not sparing the flock," and that is Satan. His representatives, discussed in verse 29, are unbelievers who come in looking and talking like Christians. You see, the world has picked up on our terminology today. They use the phrase "born again" (John 3:3) and talk about being a Christian with ease.

People in the world will talk about Jesus and sing about Jesus. They talk about the Bible and sing songs with words from the Bible. Why? Because not only is it fashionable today to give an image of being religious, but there is a very large and growing Christian market of believers who will buy everything from music to a new muffler if you say you are a Christian or have the sign of the fish on your business card!

All these wolves need to do is show up in church a couple of times a week, acting and talking just like the rest of the sheep, being very religious as they talk about love and unity. Slowly but surely, they inject their false teaching and wrong attitude into the minds of those they befriend, causing strife and division in the congregation.

## Deceived and Deceiving Others

In verse 30, Paul says, "Also of your own selves," or *out of the ministry*, "shall men arise..." The word "arise" speaks of pride, and here we see the other, more vicious tactic that the devil uses to try to destroy a local church – he uses a believer who gets puffed up in pride.

To me, one of the greatest tragedies in the church is when a person, just getting started in the ministry, has a great victory, sees a great move of God in their lives, and then tries to get ahead of God by promoting themselves.

I've seen this happen often, too: Someone will have a tremendous spiritual experience or success in an area of ministry, and then they decide they're ready to pastor a church. So they call themselves into the ministry, establish a church somewhere, and fall flat on their face.

One victory does not make a ministry! Every believer can have signs and wonders follow them if they believe and act on God's Word (Mark 16:17), but being called into full-time ministry is a sovereign act of God. And it bears repeating again and again that if God doesn't promote you, then you're not promoted.

*If you call yourself into the ministry, then you've got to keep yourself in the ministry.* And it's hard enough to be in the ministry with God backing you, but without Him it is nearly impossible, and very miserable!

The Bible says to "humble yourselves therefore under the mighty hand of God, that he may exalt you in due time" (First Peter 5:6). In other words, when you're faced with a choice to take the high road (exalting yourself) or the low road (humbling yourself), choose the low road.

Let the Lord promote you! You say, "What should I do, then?" Hide behind the Word of God. Just preach and teach the Word and let the Lord open up the doors for you.

A powerful passage of scripture about this is in First Samuel 15:17. Samuel has come to confront Saul, who has disobeyed the Lord's command by not killing Agag, the evil king. Samuel's heart is broken over Saul's disregard for the Lord's command, and he says, *"When thou wast little in thine own sight, wast thou not made the head of the tribes of Israel, and the Lord anointed thee king over Israel?"*

Think of yourself as "little in your own sight." That is one of the most important things you can do as a minister. You say, "But the Bible says that I'm the righteousness of God in Him" (Second Corinthians 5:21)! That's right – *in God's sight* you are. It's great to know that that is how the Father sees you. But *in your own sight*, you are to see yourself as small.

Understand something: God didn't lower Jesus; Jesus *"made himself* of no reputation, and took upon him the form of a servant, and was made in the likeness of men: And being found in fashion as a man, *he humbled himself*, and became obedient unto death, even the death of the cross. Wherefore God also hath highly exalted him, and given him a name which is above every name" (Philippians 2:7-9).

Do you want God to exalt you? Then humble yourself. Not only is taking the low road easier in the long run, but you will defeat any temptation to become like the believer who "arises" with pride. When this happens, they become deceived and can be used by Satan to deceive others in the congregation.

Second Timothy 3:13,14 says, "But evil men and seducers shall wax worse and worse, deceiving, and being deceived. But continue thou in the things which thou hast learned and hast been assured of, knowing of whom thou hast learned them."

Paul is telling Timothy, "If you want to keep from being deceived, continue to study the Word of God and follow after those who are faithfully teaching you God's Word." Without knowledge of the Word of God, a believer can easily be deceived.

To be deceived means to believe a lie is the truth. The lie can be a false doctrine, a false prophecy, a supernatural experience originating from demons and not the Holy Spirit, or a thought or idea that does not come from God.

When a false teacher or prophet rises up within a church, it is more grievous than when a wolf enters in from the outside, because those who are doing the damage are children of God. Although they are born again and have been filled with God's Spirit, they choose to believe what they want to believe instead of heeding warnings from the Holy Spirit and living according to the Word of God.

It's sad to say, but many of these people genuinely believe that what they are doing is right, that they are on a divine mission to free the Body of Christ from some misconception or bondage.

However, Satan's purpose is to use them to distract other believers with false doctrine, "seducing spirits and doctrines of demons." In some cases they pull congregational members away from the faith and the local church, while building their own ministry empire.

One important point I need to mention here is that there are many solid ministries of integrity who have meetings outside the local church, but their purpose is to *add to what the local church is already accomplishing in a church member's life.*

These ministries do not seek to draw people away from the local church, but they encourage believers to get involved in a local body of believers, and to use the knowledge of the Word of God that is being taught at their meetings in their own church.

# There's Nothing New Under the Son

"Also of your own selves shall men arise, *speaking perverse things*...." There are a lot of people today preaching and teaching things that they call revelation knowledge, but they are really "speaking perverse things." In essence, they are taking the Word of God and twisting it to teach their own "new and exciting revelation." They use God's Word to exalt themselves.

One of the tactics of the devil is to pressure ministers to come up with something new, exciting, or funny for their people to hear. This leads them to manufacture their own revelations, or they take someone else's sound teaching, and in trying to make something sensational out of it, they end up "speaking perverse things."

Actually, there are only a certain number of doctrines in God's Word, but it will take eternity for us to know the depth and breadth of each one. Recently, I taught a series on all the things God gave to us at the new birth. I limited the series to a certain number of weeks because of time constraint, but we could have spent years teaching on this one subject. It will take eons of time just to understand the vastness of this one doctrine!

The Bible says, "That in the ages to come he might shew the exceeding riches of his grace in his kindness toward us through Christ Jesus" (Ephesians 2:7). When I hear a minister say he's got a new revelation from the Word of God, something no one has ever preached before, I wonder if he's trying to promote himself rather than the message, because God is going to spend eternity just telling us about one simple doctrine: His grace!

Verse 30 also mentions that another reason ministers fall into the trap of trying to preach something new and exciting is to "... draw away disciples after them," or to draw crowds. Some people think that if a minister draws great numbers of people, he must be legitimate. But numbers do not make a ministry. *Truth makes a ministry.* Integrity in word and deed make a ministry.

I'd rather have five people following me as I preach the truth, rather than five thousand people following me as I "speak perverse things." Also, notice that the verse goes on to say, "to draw away disciples *after them*," – not Jesus.

This verse describes those who distort the Word to make it sensational, hoping to draw disciples away from the church and unto themselves. They're building their own kingdom, not God's. And, needless to say, if a minister's objective is to begin a church by drawing another church's members away, their priorities and their motives are wrong as well.

## Despising Government

In a similar passage of scripture beginning in Second Peter 2:9, Peter addresses the same problem. "The Lord knoweth how to deliver the godly out of temptations, and to reserve the unjust unto the day of judgment to be punished." Here, the "unjust" refers to the wolf who enters into the church from the outside, the unbeliever who acts like a believer in order to divide and destroy the church.

Peter then goes on to say, "But chiefly them that walk after the flesh in the lust of uncleanness, and despise government. Presumptuous are they, self-willed, they are not afraid to speak evil of dignities." This verse describes the believer who rises up in pride within the church. Here, we will see how a believer becomes a false teacher or false prophet.

Verse 10 begins with "But chiefly," which means that it is far worse to deal with a false teacher or prophet (believer) than a wolf (unbeliever), and that it is more grievous to be persecuted by a Christian than an unbeliever. *You will find in the ministry that your worst enemies will be other believers who are out of fellowship with God.* Why? Because they are the most miserable people on earth.

You see, an unbeliever can sin and go against God and not feel convicted. This is their nature. But a believer has the Spirit of God and a new, regenerated spirit inside them that are in continual conflict with the carnal desires that are controlling them ("that walk after the flesh in the lust of uncleanness").

The carnal believer is trying to get satisfaction from giving in to the flesh, but the only thing that will ever satisfy is returning to fellowship with the Lord and walking day by day with God. Out of fellowship with the Lord, they are constantly frustrated and miserable.

They may act like everything is alright, but they are putting on a big act, and inside they know it. They walk "after the flesh in the lust of uncleanness (not restraining physical appetites, whether for sex, money, fame, food, drink, etc.), and *despise government.*"

Now we come to the root of the problem – they cannot take instruction or submit to authority – they "despise government." Carnal believers are out of fellowship with God because they will not submit themselves to those whom God has placed in authority over them. By resisting and rebelling against authority, they are resisting and rebelling against God, who established those authorities.

Because carnal believers have no intimate relationship with the Father and avoid confrontation of their sin by the Word of God, they are totally insecure. Jesus said that they have "no root in themselves" (See the parable of the sower, Matthew 13:18-23). This means that the foundation of the Word of God is not in their lives. They have nothing to stand on.

Consequently, when it comes to choosing the Word of God or their own ideas and fleshly desires, believers who have no true security in God will go with their carnal thinking and ways. This puts them in a position to be deceived and to deceive others, to "arise and speak perverse things."

However, a believer who is secure in God, who "studies to show himself approved" (Second Timothy 2:15) and knows who he is in Christ, is secure with men; he has no problem with submitting to the authority of others because he knows who he is in God.

There are also those immature believers who may not know the Word of God well enough to understand that their attitudes are self-centered and self-seeking. These misguided and misled sheep may really believe that they are following the Lord, when in reality they are following their own thoughts or feelings rather than submitting to those in authority.

The Word of God says that we are to obey all those in authority over us, unless we are asked to do something that clearly violates the Word of God (see Chapter Eleven). And we have seen how, through the principle of delegation, the Holy Spirit will work through a chain of command (see Chapter Five).

When you go against an elder, you go against the pastor who gave him his authority. When you rebel against the pastor, you rebel against Jesus Christ, who gave the pastor His authority – and on up to God the Father, the source of all authority.

Does rebelling against God the Father's authority sound familiar? This is exactly what Lucifer did! And when Lucifer rebelled, declaring that he would exalt his throne above God's (Isaiah 14:13,14), he became Satan, God's adversary. When you rebel against God-given authority, you are acting in league with His adversary, the devil. And the Bible says that the root of rebellion is pride (First Timothy 3:6).

The verse goes on to say, "Presumptuous are they, self-willed, they are not afraid to speak evil of dignities." This is what happens when believers go against the Word of God in order to satisfy their own selfish desires. They become presumptuous (think they know more than the pastor), self-willed (their way is better than the pastor's), and they are not afraid to speak evil of dignities (they will gossip and malign the pastor and others who are God's anointed and appointed leaders).

These believers are in open rebellion against the pastor and the Word that is taught. So you say, "But what if a minister or pastor is out of line or teaching error?" Pray about it and speak to him privately, with an attitude of submission. Don't speak about it in rebellion or talk about it with others! Then leave the issue in God's hands. He will either change the situation, change you, or move you to another church.

Years ago there were some ministries that I felt would not last long, because I did not agree with some of the things they were doing. I did not agree with their doctrines or methods of running their ministries. If it had been up to me, they would have been down the tubes right then. But you know, today they are still going strong.

Of course, I am not talking about ministers committing adultery, stealing money, or blatantly deceiving people. Even the Apostle Paul spoke out about these types of sins (Second Timothy 2:17,18 4:14).

But the closer you get to ministers and their ministries, you find out they *all* have problems and weak areas, because everybody is still human. But I've learned that you don't speak against them, because they are God's anointed, His children, and He's working in them and through them just like He's working in and through you. You pray for them, reminding yourself that you, too, have weak areas!

Remember, who is the accuser of the brethren? Satan is, and when you accuse the brethren, you are falling in league with him. Like Satan, these rebellious ones, who don't understand or respect authority, who have been deceived and are deceiving others, are always looking for a way to be on top. They try to manufacture their own calling, ministry, and position in leadership, but Satan's hidden agenda is to use them to divide and disrupt the church they attend.

## The Rod and the Staff

At this point you may be saying, "How do I handle situations like this? What do I do when I see a wolf in my congregation? And, how do I keep from getting paranoid about these things, from seeing a wolf or a false teacher or prophet in every troubling situation that comes up? Is there some way of preventing all this?"

Paul goes on to say in Acts 20:31, "Therefore *watch, and remember,* that by the space of three years I ceased not to warn every one night and day with tears." A pastor, like a faithful shepherd, is to *watch* over the sheep diligently, *remembering* that the Bible warns of possible attacks from within and without the church.

A pastor shouldn't suspect everyone, but he is also not to be oblivious to signs that a deceiver or a wolf is at work among his people. Like a faithful shepherd, he should remain alert for strange doctrines, ideas, or practices that are circulating in the congregation, and be aware of the ministries that pass through town.

The Bible speaks of two things that a shepherd uses as he watches over his flock, a rod and a staff. *The staff is for the sheep.* It has a crook in it so that when a sheep gets caught in the rocks or bushes, the shepherd just hooks them around the neck and lifts them right out. *The rod is for the wolves.* It is a club to beat the wolves until they go away.

The Word of God is the pastor's staff. Second Timothy 3:16,17 says, "All scripture is given by inspiration of God, and is profitable for doctrine, for reproof, for correction, for instruction in righteousness: That the man of God may be perfect (mature), thoroughly furnished unto all good works."

Whether one member has gone astray and a counselor or the pastor speaks the Word of God to them privately, or many members have been influenced and the pastor is led to teach on the subject that is being distorted, speaking God's Word is the most effective destroyer of "seducing spirits and doctrines of demons."

Again and again, the Bible emphasizes the importance of knowing God's Word, that people perish due to the lack of knowledge. By preaching and teaching the Word of God week after week, by "holding nothing back" and giving his congregation "the whole counsel of God," a pastor is showing the greatest compassion and concern for his congregation.

An important point to mention here, too, is that one of the most crucial prayers a pastor prays for his congregation is *after* his sermon, not before it. In Colossians 4:12, Paul commends Ephaphras, the pastor of the church at Colosse, who is "always laboring fervently for you in prayers, that you may stand perfect and complete in all the will of God."

Most pastors pray before the service. They pray for their messages to be powerful and anointed, for the Holy Spirit to move during the services in a mighty way. But Epaphras also prayed after the people heard the Word of God. He prayed that they would become mature and successful by living what they had heard.

Knowledge of the Word of God builds a hedge of protection around a believer's life (Hebrews 4:12), causes discernment of good and evil (Hebrews 5:14), and when a believer goes astray, the pastor gently places God's Word around his neck to bring him back into the fold.

The rod is the exercise of the pastor's authority over those who want to divide and destroy his congregation. Paul told Titus, "For there are many unruly and vain talkers and deceivers, specially they of the circumcision. Whose mouths must be stopped, who subvert (overturn) whole houses (churches), teaching things which they ought not, for filthy lucre's (money) sake... *Wherefore, rebuke them sharply*" (Titus 1:10,11,13a).

There have been times when I have used my pastoral authority to tell false prophets to be quiet when they began to prophesy, disrupting the flow of the Holy Spirit during the service. On some occasions, I have had to instruct the ushers to remove them from the auditorium.

There have been times when I have had to tell a member of the congregation that they may attend the services, but they may not participate in a ministry capacity in any area of the church, because they have used their ministry position to extort money from members of the congregation.

I have had the painful duty of firing members of the staff who have gotten caught up in sin or strange doctrines, and many of the members of the church were being hurt by their ministry.

But David said of the Chief Shepherd, "...thy rod and thy staff, *they comfort me*" (Psalm 23:4). The sheep are comforted knowing that the shepherd carries both the rod and the staff. And a congregation develops a confidence and security knowing that not only is their pastor faithful to pray over them and give them the Word of God, but he will not hesitate to stop a wolf or a false teacher or prophet if they try to infiltrate the church.

There is great comfort for the people if their pastor will *watch and remember.*

# Chapter Seven
# Paul's Final Words and Departure

And now, brethren, I commend you to God, and to the word of his grace, which is able to build you up, and to give you an inheritance among all them which are sanctified.

I have coveted no man's silver, or gold, or apparel.

Yea, ye yourselves know, that these hands have ministered unto my necessities, and to them that were with me.

I have shewed you all things, how that so labouring ye ought to support the weak, and to remember the words of the Lord Jesus, how he said, It is more blessed to give than to receive.

**Acts 20:32-35**

PAUL BEGINS THIS PART of his message by saying, "And now, brethren, I *commend you* to God...." The word "commend" actually means "to make a deposit." He says, "Men, you have been entrusted to me for the last few years, but now I'm getting ready to leave. So I deposit you with God, and not only with God, but also *with the word of His grace.*"

As a pastor, you have the right to deposit your people "with God and the word of His grace" just as Paul did with these pastors. After you have opened up the Word of God and taught them everything that God has given you, you can place them squarely in the care of the Word you have given them.

However, this is very important: you can only deposit people into what you teach, into the Word you've given them. In other words, if you don't teach them about the new birth,

71

then you cannot believe God for their salvation. If you don't teach them the doctrine of righteousness, you cannot expect them to live according to it.

Paul preached grace, so he could deposit them into "the word of His grace." And because he taught them about trusting the Lord, he could deposit them into the hands of the Lord.

This is a great principle to remember, especially for evangelists. It's often impossible to stay with somebody and help them grow spiritually after they are saved and delivered. You can recommend a good church to them and turn them over to pastors, but a demon can still whisper to you that they'll never make it.

Satan will taunt you and say, "You bring them into the kingdom and then you leave them all alone, knowing nothing. Sure, they were healed, but they'll lose it in a week. So their craving for drugs is gone now. Just give them a few days and they will be on the streets again."

That's when you declare that, according to God's Word, you are depositing them into the hands of God and to the word of His grace. You remind the devil that the Holy Spirit can lead many other believers to minister to them. You've done your part, and now you can have peace that God will take care of the rest. After all, if He was faithful enough to bring you across their path, He will be faithful to bring whoever else is needed.

Paul was faced with this situation, because he could not stay in Ephesus and encourage and counsel these pastors forever. Therefore, he deposited them "to God, and into the word of His grace, *which is able to build you up....*"

By doing this, Paul has placed these pastors in far better hands than his own. "The word of His grace," which he has poured into these ministers, will be present to edify and build them up long after Paul has departed. And where Paul would probably disappoint and fail them from time to time, the Word of God and His grace will never fail them.

Also, after the pastors of Ephesus impart "the word of His grace" to their congregations, they, like Paul, must remember to deposit their congregations into the Word they have preached. The message of the grace of God that will keep these pastors will also keep their people as they all go through the difficult times ahead. The grace of God can carry them farther than any one minister could!

## Financial Integrity

In verse 32, Paul brings out that there is a special reward for pastors, "an inheritance among all them which are sanctified." (We'll study this in Chapter Ten.) Then he continues by saying, *"I have coveted no man's silver, or gold, or apparel."*

Why would Paul make such a statement? Because he had been given silver, gold, and apparel! On many occasions, he received many costly and precious gifts of love and appreciation as he ministered to the people.

People can get so blessed when you minister that they want to give you something valuable to show how grateful they are to God for your ministry. This is one of the aspects of the ministry that is a blessing, but it also bears a great responsibility. The minister must guard his heart to keep from coveting these things.

When Paul tells these pastors not to think that he ever coveted any of these gifts, he is setting a standard for financial integrity in ministry. Because money is one of the most important and sensitive areas in a church, I don't think it was an accident that he chose to discuss finances in the ministry just before he said farewell.

One of Satan's favorite ways to destroy a church is through mismanagement of, or sin in, finances. He particularly likes to lead a pastor or minister astray, either through ignorance or through covetousness, and then glowingly expose it to the whole world.

With the vast media coverage of every scandal in the Church that occurs today, it is vitally important that every church and every minister keep their financial affairs legally and morally in order.

One of the ways we do this in the church I pastor is to have a yearly audit by a well-known and highly respected financial firm in town. We use this annual report at the church's yearly business meeting and distribute it to all of our members. In this way, we have a current accounting for every penny if and when the staff, the congregation, the government, or the public wants to see it.

A yearly audit is somewhat costly, but it is well worth the peace of mind to the pastor and his congregation. If you are a small church and cannot afford an audit, I would urge you to keep your books straight and be open about them with your congregation. Or perhaps you have someone in your congregation who would volunteer their time for this task. The important thing is to make sure that the finances of the church are legally in order and readily available.

It is also important that you as the pastor set the standard for moral integrity in finances. The focus of your ministry should always be to minister to the people, not to get the people to minister to you with their finances.

A pastor must teach his congregation what the Word of God has to say about prosperity and giving as part of the whole counsel of God. This is teaching the people how to live in God's system of prosperity and it is essential for their success in the Christian life.

However, if a minister begins to major on finances whenever he teaches and is constantly nagging for money, his priorities are out of line. You will find that if you minister to the people and get their needs met, they will want to give something back. You will not need to pressure them.

One fact I always remember whenever there's a financial need in the church is, again, that the people are not my sheep. I've been hired by their Owner to watch over and feed this portion of His people, but the ultimate responsibility is His.

Therefore, I go to Him and say, "Lord, *You've* got a problem here. I've been faithful to feed Your sheep Your Word, and You told me in Your Owner's Manual that You would supply all my needs according to Your riches in glory by Christ Jesus. So You tell Your people what they should do. They know Your voice, and they respect Yours a lot more than they do mine!"

In this way, you don't have to keep pressing and pressing the congregation to give money all the time. Teach them about giving, pray for them, and then the responsibility is not on you; it is between the people and God. Always remember that you are called, promoted, and prospered by God, not by men.

Paul goes on to tell the pastors that they *"know that these hands have ministered unto my necessities..."* He is reminding them that there have been times when the ministry did not support him financially, and he had to find a secular job.

While he was in Corinth, Paul made tents in order to support himself while he preached to the wealthy Corinthian believers. He is making a very important point here to these pastors. Probably, some of them either didn't want to get a job or were too proud to work, because they wanted to be in full-time ministry immediately.

Pastors ask me, "When should I go into full-time ministry and give up my secular job?" I always tell them, "When the church is able to support you financially. When it can pay all your bills."

Many ministers feel it is below their dignity to go out and get a job, but Paul is saying that he not only supported himself, but his whole ministry team: "Yea, ye yourselves know, that these hands have ministered unto my necessities, *and to them that were with me.*"

When starting a new work, it may not only be a financial necessity to have an outside job, but a reassurance to the people you begin with. You are showing them in a tangible way that money is not your motive in beginning a church. You are telling them that you are just as committed to the church as any of the members.

When the church brings in enough income to support the pastor, he can and should make his income from the preaching of the Word of God. At this point, the pastor's ministry of the Word of God becomes just as demanding as any other job he may have had (see Chapter Nine). He puts maximum effort into the study of the scriptures and carrying out the vision of the church (First Thessalonians 2:9-12).

After all, if the pastor does not value the study and teaching of the Word of God as a worthy profession, neither will his congregation. Therefore, as soon as enough money is coming in regularly to pay his bills, the pastor should take this as his salary and quit any other jobs he has.

All this should be done openly and honestly before the people, and they will be proud that the church has grown to where their pastor can be fully supported.

## The Heart of a Pastor

It's interesting to note that nowhere in the gospels is it recorded that Jesus said that "it is more blessed to give than to receive." However, Paul quotes Jesus as saying this in verse 35: "I have shewed you all things how that so labouring ye ought to support the weak, and to remember the words of the Lord Jesus how he said, *It is more blessed to give than to receive.*"

This statement has been handed down to Paul from one of the apostles or followers of Jesus while He was on earth, and Paul is fully satisfied that this was what Jesus said.

It is important to notice that just before he steps upon the ship to sail away, Paul is led of the Holy Spirit to leave these pastors with this particular quote from Jesus. Paul's very last words to them deal with keeping their hearts pure in the area of finances.

A minister's heart is kept pure when his focus is on meeting the needs of the people, but a minister's heart is defiled when he begins to look for ways to get money out of the people, when he will even take advantage of the poor and weak to meet the budget of his church or ministry.

Paul is saying, "If you begin looking for what the people can give to you, instead of what you can give to the people, your heart is wrong. Remember that Jesus said, 'It is more blessed to give than to receive.'"

Unfortunately, there are some ministers today who are using the gospel for personal gain. Others have ministries that have grown so large, they have resorted to fund-raising tactics to enable them to finance the machinery of their ministries.

These ministers take verses of scripture, many times out of context or to an extreme, and use them to motivate believers into giving into their ministry. They have forgotten that their hearts should be toward giving to the people, rather than receiving from them.

When a pastor recognizes that some of his congregation are being taken in by these unscriptural teachings, he must defend his sheep with the staff, the Word of God (see Chapter Six). Teach the Word, and let the people see for themselves how God's financial system works, when to give and not to give, and how to give.

If it is necessary to expose the error in certain ministries, then let the Word of God do the exposing. Exhort your people to love and pray for the minister, then teach the Word on the subject and let the Bible be the judge of their financial practices.

Today, with highly publicized accounts of the financial misdeeds of ministers, an important passage of scripture for all of us to remember is found in First Kings, chapter 19. Here, Elijah becomes discouraged and complains to God that he is the only one in Israel who is serving the Lord. Sometimes when ministers fall, it becomes such a media event that it seems as though all ministers are corrupt, that very few have hearts for God and serving the people.

But God corrected Elijah, informing him that there were still over seven thousand more in Israel who were serving the

Lord (First Kings 19:18). And I am convinced today that for every minister who falls, there are many, many more serving God with all their heart, soul, mind, and strength.

It is important for pastors to remind their congregations of Elijah when sensationalized media reports try to discourage believers. Remind them that no matter what Elijah had seen, heard, or thought, God's Word prevailed – seven thousand had not bowed their knee.

The heart of the pastor should be a mirror reflection of the heart of Jesus, the Chief Pastor, Who loved us so much that He gave His life to save us. One of the ways I have come to recognize those who are called to pastor is by the tremendous love for people that pours out from deep in their hearts. They are constantly giving to others, and their chief desire is to see people's needs met.

This is one of the reasons that pastoring is such a rewarding and fulfilling calling. Pastors are extremely blessed because "It is more blessed to give than to receive," and true pastors have hearts that want to give and give! And, as we have said before, when the needs of the people are being met, they joyfully want to give into the ministry in return.

## An Emotional Farewell

Now we come to Acts 20:36-38, which relates Paul's farewell and his departure for Jerusalem. Again, he and these elders believe that they will not see each other after this, and it is a very emotional time for all of them.

**And when he had thus spoken, he kneeled down, and prayed with them all.**

**And they all wept sore, and fell on Paul's neck, and kissed him.**

**Sorrowing most of all for the words which he spake, that they should see his face no more. And they accompanied him unto the ship.**

I want you to notice how emotional these ministers are, and how demonstrative they are about their feelings for Paul. These verses clearly show that ministers can and should express emotions.

Over and over again I teach that pastors are human, that they have a gift to teach the Word, but they must live it like every believer. Well, pastors have emotions, too! And while we do not live according to them, but according to the Word of God, we can nevertheless express them when it is appropriate.

Some pastors believe that they must always be strong for their congregation, and that they will appear successful before other ministers if they maintain a certain distance. But it is ironic that the strongest and boldest – because they know who they are in Christ – are not afraid to show their emotions or to be affectionate with their people and with other ministers.

I believe that the Holy Spirit included these verses to encourage tenderness and affection among ministers. Paul and the pastors of Ephesus were open and honest with one another in all respects. As the pastors of Ephesus wept, hugged Paul, and kissed him good-bye, they had no problem expressing their sorrow about his leaving or their love for him, nor were they concerned about their personal reputations because they expressed their feelings. After all, pastors should walk in the liberty of the Holy Spirit more than anybody!

## Chapter Eight
# The Shepherd and His Sheep

The elders which are among you I exhort, who am also an elder, and a witness of the sufferings of Christ, and also a partaker of the glory that shall be revealed:

Feed the flock of God which is among you....

First Peter 5:1,2

UP UNTIL NOW, WE'VE BEEN LOOKING at what Paul had to say to the pastors at Ephesus in Acts 20:17-38. Now, we turn our attention to what Peter has to say to pastors in First Peter 5:1-6.

The Book of First Peter is addressed to "the strangers scattered throughout Pontus, Galatia, Cappadocia, Asia, and Bithynia" (First Peter 1:1). The "strangers" are born-again Jews who are living in these Gentile countries. They were Jewish merchants and businessmen who had left Palestine in order to make a better living, and they received Jesus as their Messiah through Christian missionaries. Peter is writing to encourage them in their new-found faith.

The words of Peter to the *pastors* of these scattered Jews are found in First Peter 5:1-6, and are closely linked with the words of Paul to the pastors of Ephesus in Acts 20:17-38. Although Paul is speaking primarily to Gentile pastors, and Peter is speaking primarily to Jewish pastors, they both cover the same basic areas.

In chapter 5, verse 1, Peter addresses, "The *elders* which are among you," just as Paul "sent to Ephesus, and called the *elders* of the church" in Acts 20:17.

81

Peter goes on to say, "who am also an elder." The Greek word for "elder" here is *sumpresbuteros,* which means "fellow elder." Even though he is an apostle, like Paul, Peter identifies himself as a fellow minister and a fellow pastor.

In Acts 20:32, Paul referred to the pastors from Ephesus as his "brethren." I want you to notice that neither Peter nor Paul set themselves above the rest of the pastors, although it is obvious that they are exhorting and encouraging them as spiritual fathers.

Peter acts as a spiritual father when he says that he is "a witness of the sufferings of Christ," which is his own testimony that he was there when Jesus was beaten and crucified. The phrase "and also a partaker of the glory that shall be revealed" is referring to his being present with Jesus on the Mount of Transfiguration.

With James and John, Peter had personally witnessed the supernatural appearance of Elijah and Moses, and he saw Jesus transfigured into all of His glory right before his eyes. (See Matthew 17:1-3).

After sharing this testimony, Peter gets right to the point in verse two when he says, *"Feed the flock of God which is among you...."* This is the same exhortation that Paul gave to the pastors of Ephesus in Acts 20:28. Paul and Peter both emphasize that the most important responsibility of the pastor is to feed the sheep, to preach and teach the Word of God to the congregation.

This verse also brings out something else that's very important: a pastor has only *one flock.* Peter says, *"the* flock which is among you." It is unscriptural to have two flocks, three flocks, or to be the pastor over more than one church on a permanent basis.

Now there is nothing wrong with a pastor of one church starting another church, or a missionary may oversee several churches for a period of time. But in these cases, they should find a pastor for the other church or churches as soon as possible, because God has called one pastor to one body of believers.

The Word of God compares the pastor and the local church to three different examples: Jesus and the universal Church; the head and the body; and a husband and a wife. Is Jesus the Chief Shepherd over more than one flock? Is a head attached to more than one body? Is a husband married to more than one wife? No! Neither should a pastor oversee more than one congregation.

## Peter Remembers

Where did Peter get that phrase, "Feed the flock of God"? Let's go back to John, chapter 21, where Jesus said to Peter:

> Simon, son of Jonas, lovest thou me more than these? He saith unto him, Yea, Lord; thou knowest that I love thee. He saith unto him, *Feed my lambs.*
>
> He saith to him again the second time, Simon, son of Jonas, lovest thou me? He saith unto him, Yea, Lord; thou knowest that I love thee. He saith unto him, *Feed my sheep.*
>
> He saith unto him the third time, Simon, son of Jonas, lovest thou me? Peter was grieved because he said unto him the third time, Lovest thou me? And he said unto him, Lord, thou knowest all things; thou knowest that I love thee. Jesus saith unto him, *Feed my sheep.*
>
> John 21:15-17

Notice that Jesus uses the word "lamb" in verse 15, and "sheep" in verses 16 and 17. That's because there is a difference between a lamb, which is a baby or newborn, and a sheep, which is an adult.

The Greek word for "feed" in verse 15 is *bosko*, and it means exactly that, "to feed." But the Greek word translated "feed" in verses 16 and 17 is *poimen*, which means "to pastor."

This is important, because when you feed a newborn lamb, you have to pick it up and put the bottle in its mouth. But with a full-grown sheep, you lead it to the grass, but it must eat on its own.

The local church is to take care of the newborns *and* the adults. Oftentimes, we find a church catering to one or to the other. For example, some churches get many people born again, but provide nothing to feed the babies or challenge the adults so they can all continue to grow. Every Sunday and Wednesday the pastor preaches an evangelistic message, but he never teaches the Word of God.

On the other hand, a pastor shouldn't offer just the meat of the Word for the adults either. At the church I pastor, we offer a class for new believers every Wednesday night, so that while I'm teaching more of the meat of the Word in the regular service, the babies can get the milk of the Word.

Like babies in the natural, new believers need a more intimate time to drink the milk of the Word, and they require a lot of personal attention. But after awhile, when they come into the main auditorium, they will begin to take little bites of the meat.

At first they will leave shaking their heads, digesting only parts of it. But as they begin to grow, you will see changes begin to take place in their lives. The Word of God will take hold in their hearts and stability and wisdom will come forth.

There is something wrong, however, if no growth is taking place in a believer's life. If you are having to put a bottle in a full-grown sheep's mouth, there is a problem with that sheep! You wouldn't put your teenager in a highchair and feed them baby food, would you? This is where the responsibility of the believer comes in. After you give them the Word, they must choose for themselves to believe it and live it.

Another point to remember is that unless you are in a very sparsely populated area, you should always have new converts in a church. I have found that no matter what message I am teaching in the regular services, the Holy Spirit will almost always weave in an evangelistic message toward the end, so that I can give an invitation for people to be saved, filled with the Holy Spirit, or restored to fellowship.

Perhaps you've heard someone say, "Jesus is coming back for a church without spot or wrinkle" (see Ephesians 5:25-27).

Some people use this verse incorrectly, implying that the Church must be perfect before Jesus comes back. Well then, He's never coming back, because we won't be perfect as long as we're continually bringing in new babies and dealing with carnal Christians who are filled with spots and wrinkles!

Also, if this interpretation of this scripture were correct, then in order for Jesus to come back, we would have to stop getting people born again and just work on ourselves. However, if the Apostle Paul said, "I count not myself to have apprehended (to lay hold of or fully appropriate every benefit of salvation) ...." (Philippians 3:13), then what makes us think we will ever become totally perfected in this life?

Full maturity will not occur in the family of God until we all get to heaven. There, "He will present us to himself a glorious church, without spot or wrinkle" (Ephesians 5:27). After the judgment seat of Christ, we will reach the unity of the faith, and the full measure of the stature of Christ (Ephesians 4:13).

In the meantime, how do you pastor all these growing, hungry lambs and sheep? You give them everything the Holy Spirit gives you from the Word. Make sure the babies are getting the "milk of the Word," and all of the sheep, young and old, are offered the meat of the Word.

Also, like natural food, when you learn about a new sauce, put it in. Every time you find a new recipe, use it. Why? Because you are adding variety and flavor so that the food is more appealing. Now I'm not telling you to sit down and make up sermons that are unscriptural and foolish just to entertain your congregation. But if God tells you to teach something a special way, then do it.

Have you ever noticed when you go to a restaurant, the way they serve the food makes it either more or less appealing, and that the atmosphere of the restaurant makes a big difference in your ability to enjoy the food? That's where praise and worship come into play. God inhabits the praises of His people, and the presence of God is the atmosphere in which the sheep will eat best.

Now some people don't find the atmosphere (music ministry) or the way the food is served (teaching of the Word) at our church to their taste. It's a matter of style, personality, etc. That's why God has different kinds of churches!

Just as different people prefer different kinds of restaurants, members of the Body of Christ prefer different ways to worship. Although we may be worshipping the same God and preaching and teaching the same Bible, the presentation is different from church to church. It is the same food, but it is prepared differently.

I have found that most great pastors today have grown up in the area in which they are called to pastor. When I was a teacher at a well-known Bible school, first-year students would come through the door declaring, "I'll never go back home!" But by graduation, God had given them a desire to take what they had learned back to their home town.

When you grow up in an area, you know how the people think, what they like and dislike, and how they communicate. You can use examples they can identify with – you know how to prepare the Word of God so that it will look good, taste good, and digest more easily! In Colossians 4:12, Paul mentions the pastor of the Colossian church, and says, "Epaphras, *who is one one of you.*"

Peter's ministry was to the Jews because his whole life's experience was among the Jewish people. And I believe one of the reasons God chose Paul to minister to the Gentiles was because Paul was a Roman citizen. He had a working knowledge of Gentile thinking and culture.

But whether the pastor is one of their own or not, it is important for a congregation to know that their pastor understands what they are going through, that he is preaching and teaching the Word of God to help them live productive, fulfilled lives. In this way, they can boldly and confidently face the challenges of the day and be an effective witness for Jesus in their city.

## The Pastor's Greatest Asset

Some pastors get the idea that *they* have the power in the church, but the people are the true power of the church. God can very easily replace pastors, but it is more difficult to replace whole congregations! Many congregations have continued to exist for long periods of time without a pastor, but no church can exist without a congregation.

The greatest asset the pastor has is not the buildings or the offerings, and it's not his preaching and teaching ability. His greatest asset is the *people*, and he must always remember that he will be held accountable for how he treats *the flock of God*.

There are some pastors who beat their sheep, and then they wonder why the flock scatters. Whenever anything goes wrong or there's not enough money, they always blame the people.

Sometimes the congregation is at fault in some area, and the pastor is led by the Spirit of God to exhort and instruct them. But his responsibility in these situations is to deal with the problem by exhorting the people in the Word of God and encouraging them to grow up spiritually (Second Timothy 3:16,17). He should correct and instruct with love and wisdom, not guilt and condemnation.

Constant bombardment of guilt and condemnation will not edify and motivate people to change. This only causes the sheep to scatter. And God will not allow His children to be beaten this way for long. He will lead them to a pastor who practices "grace thinking" (see Chapter Two), who will love them as God does and feed them well.

The pastor is the one God has appointed to lead, feed, and protect His most precious possession, His people. This is an awesome place to be! The devil loves to wake me up at four o'clock in the morning and say, "You've got all those people and all those problems and all those needs! What are you going to do? How can you possibly do it all?"

I say, "I don't know! Lord, what am I going to do?" But the Lord answers, "They are not *your* sheep, Bob! Just do what I've told you to do, by My Spirit and My Word, and let Me handle the rest." Then I can roll over and go back to sleep!

Throughout the Word of God, the shepherd never owned the sheep. *The shepherd watches someone else's sheep.* For example, Jethro hired Moses to watch his sheep; and Jesse had his son, David, watch his sheep. Pastors don't own their sheep, either.

And shepherds never tell their sheep, "You're my sheep and you've got to stay with me." No, the sheep go where the *owner* wants them to go! They submit themselves to the shepherd under whom the owner places them.

It's up to the people to find out where God wants them to be and then commit themselves to that pastor and body of believers. It's not the pastor's responsibility to tell the people where they belong. There are times when a new convert or a confused believer may need a nudge in the right direction, but what the pastor tells them should bear witness in their spirit as the leading of the Holy Spirit.

You see, all the shepherds are working for the same Boss, who is Jesus Christ, the Chief Shepherd. Through the Holy Spirit, He will tell them where to pastor, and then He will bring sheep to them, to lead and feed as He directs. Therefore, a pastor does not have to strive to make his congregation grow or hold people in his church.

Neither is the pastor supposed to turn his congregation into *his* disciples, but rather, he's supposed to teach the people how to be *disciples of Jesus Christ.* Discipleship goes into error when those in the pulpit teach that you are to become a disciple of men.

Some pastors go overboard by taking too great an interest in their congregations' lives. It's good for a pastor to care for his people and have a general knowledge of what they are facing. However, it should not matter to him what kinds of cars they drive, where they live, or how many children they have.

It is not the pastor's responsibility to go to the peoples' homes and check up on them, to make sure they are living what he preached last Sunday. Nor should he direct the elders of the church to do this.

The pastor's duty is to give the Word of God to the people, to hold nothing back and teach the whole counsel of God, and then to point them to Jesus, Who is their Owner and Chief Shepherd. He prepares the Word and makes it as appealing as possible, presents it in an atmosphere that's filled with the presence of God, and then it is up to the members of the congregation to receive it and go out and live it.

## Chapter Nine
# Taking Authority

**Feed the flock of God which is among you, taking the oversight thereof, not by constraint, but willingly; not for filthy lucre, but of a ready mind;**

**Neither as being lords over God's heritage, but being ensamples to the flock.**

**First Peter 5:2,3**

EVEN THOUGH THE SHEEP don't belong to you, Pastor, the Word of God declares that you are to "take the oversight." This means to take the authority, to stand in it and make decisions that are yours alone to make. Take it! God will not hand it to you; He commands *you* to take it.

You say, "But what if I make a wrong decision?" You'll find out soon enough, and then it's very simple to go back and make the right one! The point is, if *you* don't make the decision, somebody else will.

"But I just don't want to make waves." You are going to make waves! Most people find change difficult to handle, and sometimes cages get rattled when you set out to do God's will. But it's better to make some waves and do the will of God than to timidly sit back and try to please men.

In Acts 20:28, the Word of God declares that "the Holy Ghost hath made you overseers." If the Holy Spirit has made you an overseer, then when you take the oversight, He will reveal the direction you are to go, day by day, decision by decision. He knows the end from the beginning, and nothing takes Him by surprise!

God places the pastor in the office of chief overseer of the local church, which means He gives him the vision for that church. It is the pastor who knows the direction the church should be going. Nothing looks more silly than a leader who pulls out his hair saying, "What do I do?"

But when the pastor says, "This is what we're supposed to do," and begins to delegate responsibilities, then everybody will answer, "Yes, sir!" and start to carry them out. Why? Because the pastor is taking the oversight. He is using the ruling authority that God commands him to use, and the people will take hold of that boldness, and rest in the security that comes when they know you're doing God's will.

## A Willing Servant

No one forces you to be a pastor – you should "take the oversight thereof, *not by constraint, but willingly...*" What Paul is saying here is that you should never do anything because of pressure from men, "by constraint."

Every place I go, there is usually one pastor who will say, "Brother Yandian, I just don't understand it! My church isn't growing. People don't like me. I'm preaching the Word, I'm praying, and my family life is good. But the church is a flop."

So I ask them, "How did you come to this church?" They'll usually say something like this: "Well, I came to this little prayer group, and they prophesied over me that I was supposed to be the pastor. Then they just kept asking me and asking me, till finally I took it." Or else they will say, "I came here because the people thought I was their pastor. They voted me in one hundred percent!"

Don't ever take a position because of pressure from men. Take it because God told you. If they've waited two or three years for a pastor, they can wait for God to speak to you and give you peace about it. And just because you got one hundred percent of the vote does not mean the vote is God's will. The only way you can pastor willingly is by knowing it's God's will and not the misguided will of men for you to be there.

A pastor told me once that he didn't like pastoring, but God had forced him into it. This was his cross to bear. Every day he would pick up his cross and go to the church.

Your ministry is not your cross to bear! There may be difficult experiences and times when you have to crucify your flesh to be faithful and diligent to study and pray, but you still know that God has called you. And when God calls you to a ministry, He drops a desire for it in your heart. He doesn't call you to something you hate in order to teach you something, nor does He look down at you from heaven and laugh as you blunder through it. No! That's not God!

God will give you a deep desire to see His will fulfilled in your life and the lives of the ones He's called you to serve, and the ministry He calls you to will be an outward reflection and fulfillment of that desire. It's true that it will bring some of your greatest challenges, but it will also bring times of the greatest satisfaction.

## Freedom to Serve

Verse 2 continues: *"...not for filthy lucre, but of a ready mind."* You never take a church because the salary looks good, either! That's another way of missing God. You may be rich financially, but miserable in all other areas. Take the church because God tells you to take it, and don't make any stipulation about your salary. It's all right to find out what your salary is going to be, but if the church doesn't supply your needs, trust God to fill in the gap.

Understand something: money is good, not evil; it's *"the love of money* that is the root of all evil." (See First Timothy 6:10.) And whether you are a businessman or a minister or a housewife, you can have "filthy lucre," or an evil, covetous attitude, toward money.

The Word of God says that the right attitude toward money is to "remember the Lord thy God: for it is he that giveth thee power to get wealth, that he may establish his covenant which he sware unto thy fathers, as it is this day" (Deuteronomy 8:18).

God will prosper you and give you money because He trusts you to know what to do with it. He knows you won't just keep it all for yourself, but you will give into the gospel, because establishing His covenant in the earth is first and foremost in your mind. You don't love the money; you love God and use the money to spread the gospel.

Before I became a pastor, when I first started traveling, I came across ministers who wouldn't go to a church unless they got a certain amount of money. But some churches can't afford to bring you in, and if it's God's will for you to be there, He'll provide the difference.

I went to one church and I ended up spending more money to get there and back than I got as an offering. But when I got home, someone in the church came up to me the next Sunday, slipped $500 in my hand and said, "God told me to give you this." If you are obedient to the Holy Spirit and resist financial pressure, He will see you through!

I have also seen some pastors who treat churches as stepping stones in some grand career path they have set for themselves. They will resign one church and go to another because the pay is better.

But every position the Lord places you in should be the ultimate for you. If you are the janitor of the church – God has called you to keep the building clean – you should be content and know He'll supply all your needs. You will be the happiest, most prosperous janitor in the world, because you know you're in His will.

As a pastor, trust God to meet your needs, no matter how small or large, rich or poor, your congregation is. The Bible says to "seek ye first the kingdom of God, and his righteousness; and all these things shall be added unto you" (Matthew 6:33).

I would rather be in God's will making a little money, than out of His will making a lot of money. Money can't buy you peace, contentment, or fulfillment. Besides, if God calls you to a church, He didn't call you there to fail. Depend on Him to supply your needs as you faithfully continue preaching and teaching His Word and carrying out His vision for the church.

## Don't Muzzle the Ox

Sometimes churches read this verse of scripture ("not for filthy lucre") and they think, "Well, we don't want our pastor to be puffed up in pride, so we aren't going to pay him very much." Ironically, this is going against what the Word of God says. In First Timothy 5:17,18, Paul exhorts Timothy,

**Let the elders that rule well be counted worthy of double honour, especially they who labour in the word and doctrine.**

**For the scripture saith, Thou shalt not muzzle the ox that treadeth out the corn. And, The labourer is worthy of his reward.**

This passage of scripture is directed to those who control the pastor's salary, who are usually a board of deacons or elders in the church. Unless the church is very small, the pastor should not set his own salary.

As soon as the church is large enough and the pastor knows the members well enough to appoint those who have proven themselves faithful to the Word of God, then he should appoint a governing board under him. This provides a practical checks and balances system in case he falls in some way, provides godly counsel when he needs it, and most importantly, releases the pastor from setting his own salary.

The ones who labor in the Word and doctrine are the pastors, and "double honor" is referring specifically to money – "double honor" means "double pay." Most people think double honor should be a couple of good pats on the back instead of one! But verse 18 is a quote from Deuteronomy 25:4, which is speaking about *finances*.

In the ancient world, the ox was tied up so that he could walk around in a circle all day and tread out the corn. The farmer who wanted to keep as much corn as possible would put a muzzle on the ox, so it could not dip down and eat what was thrown on the threshing floor. But the Old Testament commanded Israel to treat their animals right. The ox was not to be muzzled.

The corn represents finances, and the ox is the pastor, locked up in his office, going around and around all day: study, pray, preach; study, pray, preach; study, pray, preach!

When the finances are brought in, the Word of God says that you shouldn't put a muzzle on the pastor. Let him "be counted worthy of double honor ... for the labourer is worthy of his reward." This is saying that being a pastor is not only a calling, but it is an occupation. Studying, praying, and preaching is the way he earns his living.

How often are secretaries in secular businesses paid better than pastors? The church does not want the pastor to dip down and take any money, so they put a muzzle on him. But the Word of God says not to do that, because he is laboring in the Word and doctrine as a profession. *God wants the Church to understand that pastoring is not a pastime! It is just as much a full-time job as being a welder or a doctor.*

Again, when you take a church, do not take it because of the salary. If you take a church for money, you put yourself in bondage to your salary, and you become tied to the church because of the money.

But if you take a church because God told you to take it, you place yourself in His hands, and you can minister "of a ready mind," or freely. Then, as the Holy Spirit directs, teach your congregation what the Word has to say about those "who labour in the Word and doctrine"! Most congregations are so grateful to receive the Word week after week, that they want to bless their pastor in any way they can.

## The Balance of Authority

There is a balance to "taking the oversight: *Neither as being lords over God's heritage, but being examples to the flock."* Peter tells the pastors that *they can be the head of the church without being a dictator.*

When I became pastor of our church, the first thing I studied and taught was church government. In all my years in the church, I had not seen many church government situations that worked well, and I wanted to find out what the Bible had to say about it.

One of the most widespread problems that I had seen was that so often the pastor had to do what a board of elders or a superintendent told him to do. And, in some cases, he had to teach what they thought should be taught.

When I saw in God's Word and began to teach that the pastor was the head of the local church, just as Jesus is the head of the universal Church, a few cried out, "Dictator! Police state!" But most of the people were happy to have a pastor who "took the oversight."

The Holy Spirit would not tell pastors not to be dictators if they weren't the head of the local church in the first place. He admonishes pastors not to abuse the ruling authority that rightfully comes with their position as overseer of a local church.

Recently someone wrote me a letter, and they told me that I had set myself up as a dictator over the church. They had read my book on church government (see my book, **Decently And In Order**) and said that I was in error when I said that the pastor gets his authority directly from the Lord Jesus Christ.

This person said that because the five-fold ministry gifts are listed in this order: apostles, prophets, evangelists, pastors and teachers (Ephesians 4:11), the pastor should submit himself to those above him. Ultimately, they told me, each local church should have a prophet and an apostle, based on Ephesians 2:20, where it says that the church is *built upon the foundation of the apostles and prophets,* Jesus Christ himself being the chief cornerstone."

But the question then arises, "Who does the apostle submit to? Does *he* become a dictator?" And Ephesians 2:20 is not declaring that apostles and prophets *themselves* are the foundation. This verse is saying that our churches should be built upon the same foundation *of* the apostles and prophets, which is the Word of God – "Jesus Christ being the chief cornerstone."

Neither is Ephesians 4:11 setting a chain of command among the five-fold ministry gifts. The Holy Spirit is simply telling us the chronological order in which God gave these gifts to the Church.

The first office given after the day of Pentecost was the apostle who established the local church at Jerusalem (Acts 2:42). Next came prophets and the first evangelist in Acts, chapter 8. And the last offices to be placed, as local churches were established, were pastors and teachers.

Clearly, each of these offices receive their authority directly from Jesus Christ Himself, or else the scripture would have read, "And he gave some, apostles; and the apostles gave some, prophets; and the prophets gave some, evangelists;" etc. This verse says that *Jesus* gave each gift.

Also, in the verses of scripture we're looking at in this book, Peter and Paul, who are both apostles, do not formally set themselves above the other pastors and elders. In each case, they make a point of saying that they have come to exhort and encourage them, as "fellow elders" and "fellow ministers."

In other words, Peter and Paul are not telling the pastors how to run their churches. They are teaching them the Word of God and imparting practical wisdom and sound guidelines that will enable these pastors to oversee the churches themselves.

*There is nothing in the Bible that indicates that the pastor should look to anyone but the Lord Jesus Christ for final authority and direction for the church he pastors.* He should have much counsel and wisdom from those around him, but when the meetings are over, the Lord will speak to the leader. God uses leaders to speak to groups.

Nevertheless, in First Peter 5:3 the Holy Spirit exhorts pastors not to abuse their authority: "Neither as being lords over God's heritage (notice whose heritage the congregation is), *but being examples to the flock.*" You will never be a dictator to your people if you *live* what you preach and teach. Dictators over churches do not do this (see Matthew 23:4).

Your life should be merely an extension of the pulpit; the pulpit should be an extension of your life. You should be the same in the pulpit and out of the pulpit. You should run your home the same way you run the church (First Timothy 3:5).

*Your ministry doesn't begin in the pulpit, it begins when you get up in the morning!* A ministry is not something you *do*, it is something you *are*. As an example to the flock, the pastor does his best to live what he teaches. Ministers are not to point to Jesus and then live any way they want to live!

And there is nothing wrong with using yourself as an example from time to time, if you don't get puffed up in pride. Paul used himself as an example many times in the Word of God, including Acts 20:20: "And how I ... *shewed you*, and have taught you *publicly*, and from house to house."

## Voluntary Slavery

A very interesting Greek word for "minister" is *huperetes*. It actually means "an underrower." It is used in Acts 13:5 to describe Mark, who traveled with Paul and Barnabas on their first missionary journey.

In the time in which Paul lived, there were three different levels of rowers on a boat, and all the rowers were slaves. I know it may not edify you greatly to hear that as a minister you are a slave, but the ministry is not glamorous, it is work. When you choose to be a minister, you choose to become a slave to the Lord Jesus Christ.

In Second Peter 1:1, Peter makes a point of declaring that he is first a servant, which literally means "bondslave," and second an apostle, of Jesus Christ. By referring to himself as a bondslave, Peter is declaring that he has voluntarily sold his entire life to Jesus. He has no personal rights, privileges or property. Everything he has, is, or does belongs to his Lord.

Likewise Paul and Timothy, in addressing the Philippians in chapter 1, verse 1, call themselves the servants (bondslaves) of Jesus Christ, which literally means they are Jesus' property. (See also Romans 1:1 and Titus 1:1.)

Anyone who is born again automatically becomes a child of God, but a believer chooses whether or not they will become a slave, or totally sold-out, to Jesus. A minister, by definition, chooses to become a permanent slave for the Lord.

As an underrower, the lower you are, the more your oars will dip into the water and the harder it is to row. On the upper levels, your oars don't dip so deeply into the water, and the rowing is easier.

Everybody knows that those who have the best time on the boat are the ones who sit on deck and just enjoy the breeze and the sun. This is the congregation! They sit on Sundays and midweek services and enjoy the Word and the presence of God because the pastor and his helpers have been down in the bottom rowing all week!

## Establishing a Relationship

When I became pastor of our church, I had been an active member from the very first service of the church. Nearly everyone in the congregation was familiar with me, as I had taught classes and had even taught from the pulpit on a regular basis. By the time God placed me in the position of pastor, a strong relationship between the people and myself had already been established, and this enabled me to plunge right in to the teaching of church government and taking the authority God commanded me to take in the church.

But most pastors, whether they are beginning a new church or are taking over a church someone else has pastored, have the task of establishing a relationship with the people before they can take full authority. A pastor forms a relationship with his people and ultimately establishes his authority by showing them who he is and by faithfully teaching the Word of God.

No matter how bad the situation is when you become the pastor, take enough time to let the people know you and get used to your delivery of the Word of God before you begin making changes. When you first come to a church, your authority is not the issue, *you* are the issue! Authority will be received when the people know you and trust you; it cannot be forced.

After you have established a relationship, then you can begin the process of *slowly* setting policies as you teach the congregation what the Word of God has to say about the office of a pastor and church government. Clean the house slowly and prayerfully!

If there are some difficult or even corrupt people on staff or in positions of authority, draw upon the grace of God to minister to them and give you patience till the situations turn around or the Holy Spirit releases you to replace them. But establish the relationship first.

Be careful not to let those you socialize with dictate policy to you, either. When you are out with friends from the church, gently make it clear that you do not mix business with pleasure. Some may be offended at first, because they may have invited you to lunch to discuss "their agenda." But the congregation will ultimately find security in the fact that their pastor is not dictated to by his friends.

Another issue to be aware of is not to let your wife dictate policy through you. You should talk things over with her and receive her counsel, just as you can solicit and receive counsel from your close friends. However, just as you should not *take* a church "by constraint," or because of pressure from men, you should not *run* the church by the pressure from men. Your authority comes from the Lord Jesus Christ, and He is the one who will ultimately lead you.

Along these same lines, you should protect your wife and family from the church. Do not allow members of the congregation to get to you through her or your children. And your family time is family time. This is not the time to discuss church business. Keep them informed of what is going on so that they are not surprised if and when someone tells them something they should know. But assure them that church business will be handled by you at the church.

Right from the beginning, if you are not used to confrontation or have avoided dealing with conflict in the past, get in the habit of confronting people directly and privately. Some pastors avoid confrontation with one individual or a few members by preaching against them from the pulpit. This is the coward's way to handle conflict. Go to them and settle the issue privately.

When a pastor either avoids these issues or discovers that gossip is spreading throughout the congregation, he will be forced to address the problem from the pulpit, because it has affected too many people.

Some pastors are actually afraid to take the oversight, to firmly grasp the ministry God has given them and take the reins, because they fear somebody will say they are a dictator. That's like a father saying, "I'm not going to run this family; I don't want my wife and kids to think I'm a dictator." Believe me, the kids are waiting for you to take the reins, your wife is waiting for you to make a decision, and the world wants you to take charge of your family!

Many people mistake confidence in authority for arrogance. Arrogant people are self-made; confident people are God-made. When you are confident, all the glory goes to God. You can step into the pulpit and preach and teach His Word in power, knowing that it is the Word and the Holy Spirit working in you, not by your own abilities, that you will succeed.

Know where your confidence is, that you are called to pastor this church, that God will give you the grace to establish a strong relationship with the people, that He commands you to "take the oversight," and that He will give you the strength and wisdom to fulfill your calling.

Throughout the Word of God, the church is compared to two things: a body and a family. A body and a family each have one head, one who is given ruling authority. In the Body of Christ, Jesus is the head, and in the family, the husband has final authority and accountability for his family.

In the local church, the pastor is commanded to take the oversight, and he is the one who labors more in the Word of God than anyone else in his church, being a faithful example to his flock. If he does these things, he will not become a dictator, or "lord over God's heritage." He will take the oversight with compassion and integrity as God commands.

# Chapter Ten
# The Chief Shepherd Shall Appear

**And when the chief Shepherd shall appear, ye shall receive a crown of glory that fadeth not away.**

**First Peter 5:4**

WE KNOW THAT JESUS embodied all of the five-fold ministry gifts. Hebrews 3:1 calls Him "the Apostle and High Priest of our profession." In Acts 3:22,23 Peter calls Him "that prophet." From the gospel accounts, it is obvious that He preached the gospel and did the work of an evangelist. And Nicodemus called Him "a teacher sent from God" in John 3:2. But now, in First Peter 5:4, Jesus is referred to as the "Chief Shepherd," or "Chief Pastor."

As our Chief Shepherd, we can apply First Peter 5:1-3 to Him, also. We see that God didn't twist Jesus' arm to take His position as Chief Pastor over the Church, neither did we put pressure on Him. He took it "willingly, not by constraint."

Jesus didn't become head of the Church because of the tremendous salary. In fact, He gave up everything He owned to come and redeem us. Therefore, He was free to do God's will, and God supplied all of His needs!

Although Jesus has been given all authority in heaven and in earth, He is not a dictator over the Body of Christ. He allows us to choose whether or not we will follow Him, and He is the supreme example for us to follow.

## Someone To Turn To

When Peter refers to the Chief Shepherd, he is reminding these pastors that they have a Pastor over *them*. Sometimes pastors will ask me, "Will you be my pastor?" I consider that an honor. And there are times when I will call another pastor for advice and counsel, too.

But if you're stuck in the middle of nowhere and you wish you had a pastor – you do! His name is Jesus! He's the Chief Pastor, and He's always there. You will never find Him out of His office, away on an emergency, or having left instructions with the Holy Spirit that He is not to be disturbed.

In Hebrews 13:20, Jesus is called the "great shepherd of the sheep," and He is called *the Word* in John 1:1,14. Therefore, as He feeds you, you in turn can feed the congregation.

I am often asked, "Is it all right if I use your sermons?" They're not my sermons! In fact, if you try to pin me down, it may be that half of my message came from the tapes and books of other ministers. And if you asked those ministers where they got their messages, they would probably say mostly from other ministers!

We can all use what God has given others, because we realize that it all comes from the Lord. You see, God does not regularly pour new revelation into you. You read books, listen to tapes, and then meditate on the Word prayerfully, letting the Holy Spirit make the truth real to you. It will then become your own revelation.

In fact, I believe it is wrong to shut yourself off from the materials of others and expect the Holy Spirit to give you information. Revelation is built upon revelation. If you will not read good books and listen to good tapes, the Holy Spirit is not bound to "reinvent the wheel." It is when you study what He has already revealed to others that He is faithful to reveal more to your heart.

However, using someone else's material *alone* is not enough, either. While in our bookstore one day, a couple of visiting pastors were talking. One asked the other, "What reference materials do you use most of the time?" Our bookstore manager was horrified to hear, "Oh, I just listen to a cassette tape on Saturday night and preach it on Sunday morning!"

This is not only an injustice to the congregation, but to the pastor himself. It is good to listen to tapes and read books, but meditate on the material and the Word you are studying long enough to make the message your own. "*Study* to show yourself approved unto God, a *workman* that needeth not to be ashamed...." (Second Timothy 2:15).

## The Alpha and the Omega

In Revelation 1:9, the Apostle John writes, "I John, who also am your brother, and companion in tribulation...." Notice that John calls himself "a brother and companion in tribulation." Like Paul and Peter, he doesn't emphasize the fact that he is an apostle, but a fellow servant and minister of Jesus Christ.

In verses 10 and 11, John goes on to say, "I was in the Spirit on the Lord's day, and heard behind me a great voice, as of a trumpet, Saying, I am Alpha and Omega, the first and the last: and, What thou seest write in a book, and send it unto the seven churches which are in Asia; unto Ephesus, and unto Smyrna, and unto Pergamos, and unto Thyatira, and unto Sardis, and unto Philadelphia, and unto Laodicea."

The greatest Pastor in the whole world has come to visit John! In verse 12 he says, "And I turned to see the voice that spake with me. And being turned, I saw seven golden candlesticks." The seven candlesticks refer to the seven churches mentioned in verse 11.

A candlestick at this time was not a little holder with a wax candle in it. In those days they used lamps filled with oil, so each church is represented by an oil lamp. The oil represents the Holy Spirit, and God is saying that churches are to be filled with the light of the Holy Spirit, shining brightly in the darkness of this world.

Verse 13 continues, "And in the midst" – the Greek literally says, "walking around in the midst" – "of the seven candlesticks one like unto the Son of man, clothed with a garment down to the foot, and girt about the paps with a golden girdle." This, of course, is Jesus, our High Priest. It says that He was clothed magnificently with a robe down to His feet and a golden girdle, or breastplate, around His chest.

In the Old Testament, the high priest wore a breastplate with twelve stones, representing the twelve tribes of Israel. But the one that Jesus is wearing does not have the stones in it, because He is acting as the High Priest over the Church. John is watching our High Priest and Chief Shepherd of the Church walk among these seven local churches.

I want you to understand what these verses of scripture are revealing to us about Jesus today. In this passage, He is not just the meek, mild Jesus that came in the manger. This is a picture of our risen Lord Jesus, who has ascended on high and has been seated at the right hand of the Father, King of kings and Lord of lords over heaven and earth. And this is the Jesus who is walking among the churches today!

Jesus is not walking among dead, religious churches, either. He is walking among living, powerful churches that are truly lamps in this world, bringing the truth of God's Word and power to the lost and needy. And, He is walking in the midst of your church today as you preach and teach the Word of God and are led in the power of the Holy Spirit.

Verse 14 goes on to say, "His head and his hairs were white like wool, as white as snow," which symbolizes His sinless, righteous character, "and his eyes were as a flame of fire," which means that nothing escapes His vision.

Verse 15: "His feet like unto fine brass, as if they burned in a furnace;" which refers to judgment, "and his voice as the sound of many waters." Can you imagine trying to talk at the bottom of Niagara Falls? When Jesus Christ speaks, you cannot even try to object, because His Word is final authority and will drown you out completely!

Verse 16: "And he had in his right hand seven stars," which represent the seven pastors of the seven churches. We know this, because in verse 20 Jesus tells John, "The mystery of the seven stars which thou sawest in my right hand, and the seven golden candlesticks. The seven stars are the *angels* of the seven churches: and the seven candlesticks which thou sawest are the seven churches."

Most people believe from this verse of scripture that each local church must have an angel over it. I don't know if that is true or not, but I can tell you that verse 20 is not speaking of an angel from heaven.

The Greek word for angel is *angelos*, where we get the English word "angel." However, in most cases in Greek literature, it is not used to refer to an angel, but rather to a "messenger," whether from men or from God.

In James 2:25, the Bible says that Rahab the harlot received the "messengers" with peace. The "messengers," or the two spies that were sent out, are called *angelos* in the Greek.

Since *angelos* can mean "messengers that God sends," which can be either men or angels, or "messengers that men send," how do we know whether verse 20 is talking about divine angels from heaven or human beings? Let's go to Revelation 2:1-4:

> Unto the angel of the church of Ephesus write; These things saith he that holdeth the seven stars in his right hand, who walketh in the midst of the seven golden candlesticks;
>
> I know thy works, and thy labour, and thy patience, and how thou canst not bear them which are evil: and thou hast tried them which say they are apostles, and are not, and hast found them liars:
>
> And hast borne, and hast patience, and for my name's sake hast laboured, and hast not fainted.
>
> Nevertheless I have somewhat against thee, because thou hast left thy first love.

In this letter, and in all of the seven letters in chapters two and three of Revelation, Jesus addresses "the angel," or "the messenger," of that local church. But wait a minute! We know this can't be an angel from heaven because no angel has left their first love. If they had, they would no longer be serving God.

Jesus is addressing the human messengers whom He sent to oversee these churches: the pastors. In each letter, He has something against the *messenger* (or pastor) placed over each church. He lets them know where He's pleased and where He's disappointed, where they are succeeding and where they need to change. Jesus holds the pastor accountable for the spiritual growth and maturity of the local church.

I also want you to notice that there was only *one* angel, or pastor, of each church. God recognizes one pastor for each of the seven churches. And the seven stars, which Jesus indicates in Verse 20 are the pastors of the seven churches, were not in John's hand or another apostle's hand; they were not in a prophet's hand; they were in the hand of the Lord Jesus Christ.

Each believer's ministry comes from the Lord Jesus, and we are each accountable to Him. We may answer to others around us, but our ministry office comes only from Jesus, and we are in His hand of power and protection.

## His Eyes Are a Flame of Fire

Jesus walks among the churches today, which means He walks among all believers. Remember that as He walks in your midst, His eyes are a penetrating flame of fire, and nothing gets past Him. These eyes see past the outward life into the motive of the heart, where sin begins (Hebrews 4:13).

Jesus sees into the heart of every believer, but He holds the pastor accountable for the spiritual well-being of the church. First Peter 5:3 says that the pastor is to be an example to the flock, and in Revelation, chapters 1-3, it is to the pastors of the churches that Jesus speaks when He comes to exhort and correct the churches. The call to the ministry means that the pastor lives by a higher standard than the congregation. God holds him to a greater accountability (James 3:1).

Ministers, because of this greater accountability, *the sins you commit in private God will make public.* Now this may not include things that you do accidently or things for which you've repented and received forgiveness. This is whatever sins you persist in doing. If you live a double standard, preach one way and live another way, God will see to it that it is exposed.

The reason God acts so strongly in this area is because whatever sins the pastor indulges in will be found in his congregation. A church reflects the personality and life of its pastor. What he allows in his life, the people will allow in theirs.

Just as Jesus is the door for the Church (John 10:7), the pastor is the door for the local church. He allows blessing or cursing into the flock. When there is righteousness in the pulpit, there will be righteousness in the congregation. If there is immorality in the pulpit, there will be immorality in the congregation.

We have seen that the sheep are God's precious possession and are ultimately His responsibility. Therefore, He will not tolerate a wayward pastor for His people for too long. Remember, He is longsuffering, but not *infinitesuffering.*

Now what I'm talking about is not just a small area of problems – every church has those and must deal with them – and that is not necessarily a reflection of the pastorate. But when a certain sin pervades most of the congregation, it is usually because the pastor is having the same problem. Because he won't plug the holes in his own life with the Word, the devil will use those openings as doorways into the congregation.

No pastor lives everything he preaches and teaches perfectly. And the congregation can't expect him to be exactly like Jesus. But they can expect him to be faithful, to be an example for them to follow, and the chief one among them to practice what he teaches. They can expect him to live a moral, godly life before them and the world.

Sin is always selfish, and it never ceases to amaze me when a minister will admit to sinning, but at the same time acknowledge that he never thought about how his sin would hurt his family, his friends, his church, or the Body of Christ at large. Whether it is a short time of pleasure or what appears to be an easy way out of a difficult situation, in the end your sin will cause immeasurable damage to those you love.

The Word of God continually exhorts us as believers to guard our hearts against the wiles of the devil to entrap us in sin, and we do this by the Word of God. Therefore, as the feeder of the sheep, the pastor of the flock should have the greatest hedge of protection around his own heart.

Psalms 119:11 says, "Thy word have I hid in mine heart, that I might not sin against thee." And Second Peter 1:4 says, "Whereby are given unto us exceeding great and precious promises: that by these ye might be partakers of the divine nature, having escaped the corruption that is in the world through lust."

If a pastor sins in a major area and repents, the board of advisors, deacons, or elders of the church should determine a period of time before he will return to the pulpit. It has taken time for the pastor to fall into sin, and it will take time for him to renew his mind with God's Word and build new habits of thinking and behavior to replace the wrong ones.

In some cases, the hurt and outrage of the congregation may be to a degree that it is impossible for the pastor to return. However, if he truly repents and submits himself to another pastor's authority until he is fully restored, he should continue to fulfill his calling. Every hero (other than Jesus) in the Word of God was not a hero because they were perfect, but because they got back up after they fell down.

If a pastor should go into error or be overtaken in a fault and not repent, the advisory board or board of deacons or elders should have the authority to fire him. In our church, this is the practical balance of authority: the pastor chooses the members of the advisory board, but the advisory board has authority over his salary and even his position in cases of extreme sin or doctrinal heresy.

But whatever the checks and balances are in your church government, pastors must always remember that Jesus will have the final word! The pastor is called the star, but Jesus is the Sun, shining in full strength; the pastor is a voice, but Jesus is the Living Word that speaks as many waters. His voice can never be overpowered or silenced, no matter what a pastor says or does.

A life of holiness is expected and demanded by our Lord Jesus. Get rid of the image of an overindulgent Jesus Who will let you brush off sin and ignore the things you're doing! He is merciful and gracious to "forgive us and cleanse us from all unrighteousness" (First John 1:9), but don't think He doesn't care if we sin. His eyes are a flame of fire!

## The Pastor's Crown

Salvation is a *gift*, but *rewards* will be given in heaven for the works we do in God's will on this earth. The Bible talks about many different rewards in heaven, and specifically mentions a number of golden crowns.

The crown is actually a wreath, which was made of olive leaves in the Greek culture. The one who received the wreath was the person who won the race. But there won't be just one winner in heaven!

Jesus will be handing out many wreaths – made of gold that won't fade away. There won't be just one gold medal, one silver medal, and one bronze medal as we have today in the Olympic Games. The gold will be available to anyone who finishes their race.

Now we know that there will be many believers who will just get into heaven and that's it (First Corinthians 3:15). But I want to earn many eternal rewards. Don't you?

The "ye" that Peter is addressing in this verse of scripture, you remember, is the pastors. "And when the Chief Shepherd shall appear, *ye* shall receive a crown of glory that fadeth not away." So there is a crown in heaven just for pastors! It's a crown that will be given by the Lord Jesus Christ when He *appears:*

> For the Lord himself shall descend from heaven with a shout, with the voice of the archangel, and with the trump of God: and the dead in Christ shall rise first:

> Then we which are alive and remain shall be caught up together with them in the clouds to meet the Lord in the air: and so shall we ever be with the Lord.

First Thessalonians 4:16,17

Jesus will *appear* at the rapture, described in First Thessalonians 4:16,17 above, and at that grand and glorious moment the Owner is going to claim His sheep for eternity. It is at this time that He will also reward the pastors who have been faithful to feed His flocks through the Church Age.

And what are the qualifications for the pastor's crown? They are outlined in the previous verses of scripture: "feed the flock of God," "take the oversight," do these things "willingly," not for "filthy lucre's sake," and don't be a dictator, but be an "example to the flock."

The office of the pastor is unique because it is a type of the Lord Jesus Christ. As He is head over the universal Church, the pastor is head over the local church. The pastor should reflect Jesus' character and leadership, leading, feeding, and loving his flock as Jesus does the Body of Christ.

The office of the pastor is also unique within the five offices – apostles, prophets, evangelists, pastors, and teachers – because only the pastor is called to stay with one local body of believers. The other ministers go to all believers. That doesn't mean that a pastor can't travel from time to time, but his main duties and obligations are at a local church.

In the Book of Revelation, Jesus refers to the pastors as stars that He holds in His right hand (which represents strength). We know that no two stars in the heavens are the same. This means that God gives each pastor a unique vision, and no two churches are exactly alike. As stars, some are bigger

114

than others and some are more visible than others – but they all shine!

Another thing about stars is that all of them are limited in their brilliance, which means that no one church will reach the entire world. Each church has their part to play, but the moment a church says that it will encompass the whole earth, it has stepped into the shoes of Jesus Himself. He is the Sun; He is the One Who will light the whole world!

Each church should be the size and brilliance God has called them to be, thankful for the privilege of bringing the gospel to the people and making disciples for the kingdom. They should not be envious or jealous of what another church has or is doing, nor should they try to imitate others. The best thing any pastor, minister, ministry, or church can do is to be themselves and *imitate Jesus*. He's the One to keep our eyes on!

As a pastor, people pat you on the back and give you many things. I have plaques, awards, diplomas, and ordination papers all over my wall. I've got certificates from organizations that I respect highly. These things are wonderful and I'm grateful for them, but they will all fade away.

The greatest rewards will come when I stand before Jesus. And the rewards that I receive from Him will never fade away (First Peter 1:4)!

## Chapter Eleven
# God Gives Grace to the Humble

**Likewise, ye younger, submit yourselves unto the elder. Yea, all of you be subject one to another, and be clothed with humility: for God resisteth the proud, and giveth grace to the humble.**

**Humble yourselves therefore under the mighty hand of God, that he may exalt you in due time.**

**First Peter 5:5,6**

IN THESE VERSES OF SCRIPTURE, Peter is changing his focus from the responsibilities of the pastor to the responsibilities of the congregation. As we study this passage of scripture and related passages, the Word of God will give us an even clearer picture of how the local church is put together, how the people flow with the pastor and how individual believers should relate to one another.

This section begins with, "Likewise, ye younger, submit yourselves unto the elder...." Literally, this means, "Likewise, ye immature, submit yourselves unto the mature." By saying this, he's telling the congregation to submit to their pastor in spiritual matters.

This does not necessarily mean that the pastor is always smarter than anybody else; there will always be people in the congregation who are more highly educated and intelligent. But it means that pastors should stay at least one step ahead of everybody with respect to the Word of God and the things of God.

Some pastors read these verses and wrongly conclude that they are supposed to know everything about everything.

That's impossible – you can't know everything! No one can! If I need help with something on the practical or natural side of running the church, I will draw somebody in from the congregation who has expertise in that area, who can assist me or my staff in what we are trying to accomplish.

For example, when it comes to computers, all I know is how to turn the things on! So I get help from someone who knows computers, and I submit to him in that area.

My calling demands only that I be mature in the Word of God and the moving of the Holy Spirit. And, as I am faithful in this area, the congregation can confidently submit to me in spiritual matters.

## Be Clothed with Humility

Verse 5 goes on to say, "Yea, all of you be subject one to another, and be clothed with humility...." The Kenneth Wuest translation says, "Moreover, all of you, clothe yourselves with humility toward one another...."

Many Christians believe that "humility" means to be low, downtrodden, even poor. "Humility" actually means "lowliness of mind," which is an *attitude*. This attitude is best described in Romans 12:3, where we are exhorted "not to think more highly of ourselves than we ought." The key to having a servant's heart, as well as a teachable spirit, is to "clothe yourself with humility," to cultivate a *submissive attitude* at all times and in all situations.

When a believer adopts a submissive attitude toward others, whether they are dealing with their boss or their children, they become servants to all people. They don't think of themselves as being less important or more important than any other human being. They are powerfully aware at all times that God considers every person valuable, unique, and special. The opposite of a submissive attitude, of course, is *pride*.

The fastest way for a believer to stop receiving the Word of God and growing spiritually is to get puffed up with arrogance and pride, or to think of themselves as spiritually superior to their pastor and to the rest of the congregation. Prideful people are so busy nitpicking over everything the pastor says, that they are unable to receive anything from God through him.

Being "clothed with humility" is one of those disciplines in the Word of God that a believer must do himself. Like faithfulness and commitment, the pastor can preach it and teach it, but in the end it is up to the believer to choose to do it. This is self-discipline. *God established the local church to help believers become disciples (disciplined to the Word of God).*

When a person is born again, he automatically becomes a *believer,* a member of the universal Church. But to become a *disciple,* he must submit himself to instruction in a local church. Again, Jesus did not tell us to go into all the world and make "converts" of all nations. He said to make "disciples" of all nations (Matthew 28:19,20). And the purpose of the local church is to turn converts into disciples (Ephesians 4:12).

The new birth brings us out of the kingdom of Satan and sin, but discipleship gets the sins out of us. Being a child of God gives us the desire not to sin, but being a disciple causes our minds to be renewed with the Word. This causes us to walk in sanctification with God so that through Him we can overcome sin in our everyday lives.

It is often said that God delivered the children of Israel out of Egypt, but He never did get Egypt out of the children of Israel. There are a lot of Christians like that today. It is usually because they will not submit themselves (or discipline themselves) to learn from a pastor of a local church.

When a believer does not submit to a pastor and get involved in a local church, it is because of pride, and usually this prideful attitude keeps him from walking in humility toward other believers as well. Because submitting to a pastor seems beneath him, any other believer who does so will also seem beneath him. Therefore, he cannot walk in an attitude of humility toward other believers either.

The reason these believers never grow up in God is found in the rest of the verse: "... for God resisteth the proud, and giveth grace to the humble." You need the grace of God to live the Christian life and to grow up spiritually, and God only pours out His grace on "the humble," those who have a submissive attitude.

The "humble" believer *knows* that he needs God's grace to do all God has called him to do. On the other hand, the proud person believes not only can he (or should he) do everything himself, but he can (or should) do it better than anyone else.

The difference between the proud believer and the humble believer can be found in verse 6, which says, "Humble yourselves therefore under the mighty hand of God...." In scripture, the hand of God is always a symbol of the supernatural. It is the height of arrogance to think you can do what only the hand of God, the power of the Holy Spirit, can do. Therefore, in this verse, His hand represents a hand of grace.

To the believer, God's hand is an open hand, filled with all of His provision, wisdom, and strength. The humble man gladly reaches out and receives the supernatural grace of God that is extended to him. He knows that he can't succeed in the Christian life without it. He also knows that no believer deserves it, but can receive it through faith in the Word of God.

But the proud believer pictures the hand of God as being a *closed fist*. He must rely on himself to get through life. And because he sees only a closed fist, he rejects the supernatural leadership of the pastor, and the fellowship of other believers, who are all part of the *open* hand of God.

No pastor knows everything about the Word of God, and there is no perfect local church. But we have seen in previous verses of scripture, and previous chapters in this book, that the Holy Spirit will move on the pastor to speak forth whatever his people need for the moment, or even lead another member of the congregation to minister to a believer.

However, if a believer will not "be clothed with humility," if he will not submit to the pastor or receive from other believers, he will miss what God wants to give him.

After a Christian humbles himself under God's hand and receives from those God has given him, he must next obey. In this manner, he is now prepared to not only *hear* from God, but be *used* by God to minister to others.

## The Power of Submission

"Submission" is an act of our own will. We "clothe ourselves with humility toward others." *Our* responsibility is to humble ourselves under God's hand; *His* responsibility is to exalt us in due season.

All believers are directly under the hand of the Lord. We are all priests before our great High Priest, and ultimately we answer to Jesus. In other words, in eternal terms, we are *always* to be in submission to the Lord Jesus Christ.

But there are times when God commands us to submit to other people – bosses, parents, teachers – believers and unbelievers alike. Whether we like our boss or not, submission is good for us. For the few moments or hours we are under submission, we learn how to better handle authority.

For example, if a policeman is directing traffic at the intersection you are passing through, for the time that you are in that intersection, you must submit to the policeman's authority. When you are at work, you submit to your boss; but when you are at home, you are the boss. Submitting to someone you don't like or agree with helps to make you a more compassionate boss.

So we find out that submission is relative; who you submit to depends on where you are at the moment. And no matter who you are and no matter where you are, you are always in the sandwich of authority. Someone may be under you, but someone is always above. God sits at the top. The music minister is the head of the choir, but he is still submitted to the pastor; the husband is head of the family, but Christ is the head of the man (First Corinthians 11:3).

No believer is an island unto himself or his own boss, because each of us will ultimately answer to Jesus. When we submit ourselves to a pastor and commit ourselves to a local church, we are submitting ourselves to God, to His Word, and to His Spirit. And when we discipline and commit ourselves in this manner, there is no limit to what miracles God can do in our lives!

Jesus marveled at the faith of the centurion because of his simple understanding of authority: "For I am a man under authority, having soldiers under me" (Matthew 8:9). Because he understood the power of submission to authority, this centurion received a great and mighty miracle!

## Authority and Submission

The whole earth operates under a system of authority and submission, which serves to hold the world together and causes us to live in peace despite the devil's operations. Without levels of authority, chaos and confusion would reign in our lives.

The more you understand authority and submission, the more you can grow in God, because "God gives grace to the humble." If you persist in rebelling against authority, in harboring an unsubmissive attitude, you are rebelling against God, who is the Source of all authority.

Authority and submission only work among *equals*. Without equality, you only have slavery, but where equality is stressed, submission is no problem.

For example, when the husband considers his wife to be his equal and treats her accordingly, she has no problem submitting to him. Likewise, when the wife understands she is equal with her husband, she can joyfully submit to his authority and there is peace in the home.

Jesus calls us His "joint heirs." We are seated "with Him" in heaven. The work of the cross has made us equal in position to Christ. Therefore, submission to Him comes naturally. There is equality in *worth*, but hierarchy in *function*.

Throughout the Word of God, there are references to levels of authority in the local church. The mere mention of words like "bishop or overseer," "elder," and "pastor" indicates that God has set a hierarchy of responsibility in our churches to establish order and keep the peace.

A pastor, elder, bishop, or deacon is no better than anyone in the congregation. If they think so, they are headed for a fall. If the pastor stresses equality in the church, submission will have little resistance. The term "pastor" must mean there is a "congregation." "Shepherd" means there are "sheep." "Leader" means there are "followers," and "authority" means "submission" must follow.

There is no way around this fact: your pastor is "over you in the Lord" (First Thessalonians 5:12). But I want you to notice that it says "in the Lord." It does not say that your pastor is over you in your natural life. He is over you in spiritual things.

In the past we have had some distortion of the doctrine of submission and authority in the local church. In fact, today you can mention "submission" to some believers and they will close their ears and turn away in disgust or fear. This is because the doctrine of submission and authority was taken to an extreme. Because the pastor was believed to be superior, submission meant slavery.

The extreme teaching we are referring to is essentially that the pastor or a designated elder in the church has authority over church members' natural, as well as spiritual, lives. For example, each believer is expected to get approval from an elder or the pastor for every decision they make, from what car to buy to whom they should marry.

But, of course, the pastor's responsibility is to "lead and feed," to pray and carry out the vision for that local church and preach and teach the Word of God. The pastor, and the staff of elders, bishops and deacons who serve him, are "over" the congregation only in spiritual things.

Just from a practical standpoint, I have a twenty-four-hour-a-day job trying to live the Word of God myself! It would be impossible for me and our staff to try to follow everyone in our congregation around to make sure they were living it, too.

If members of the congregation are having difficulty making decisions in certain areas of their lives, it goes without saying that the church doors should be open for them to come and receive godly counsel and advice that is in line with the Word of God. But again, the pastor or a staff member would be giving *counsel, not commands.*

First Thessalonians 5:12 says that my job is to "admonish" the people, or put them in remembrance of God's Word. It does not say I dictate to them. A dictator's view of authority and submission remove equality from the system. And *without equality, submission and authority become a system of slavery.* As a result of this movement, some believers have turned a deaf ear to the scriptural doctrine of submission and authority and have gone to the other extreme, which is rebellion.

These believers, in their hurt and disillusionment, choose to wander from church to church, refusing to submit to the leadership of a pastor. They have a resentful attitude toward all authority, assuming that any authority is corrupt. As a result, they cannot grow in God, and so they become even more frustrated and bitter.

Others, after being "burned" by one pastor, find it difficult even to trust God to lead them to another church where they can feel free to submit and commit themselves. They are brokenhearted and need to be healed.

That healing will come as they ask God to show them what local body of believers is their church home, submit themselves to a pastor, and "put their hand to the plow" to work. If they will do this, not only will they begin to grow again spiritually, but they will place themselves in a position to be mightily blessed of God. If we humble ourselves under the mighty hand of God, He will exalt us.

## The Enemy of Humility

Pride, the enemy of humility, is the opposite of a submissive attitude. Pride occurs when you elevate yourself above someone else for any reason. If Satan can cause a pastor or a congregation to enter into pride (thinking themselves to be better than others), he can destroy that body of believers.

There are two areas where believers can view themselves as better than others: in spiritual things and in natural things. Spiritual pride is called *bigotry*, and natural pride is called *prejudice.*

*Bigotry is an intolerance toward other believers who do not believe what you believe about a certain area of the Word of God.* For example, there are many churches today who do not believe in speaking with tongues. They interpret the scriptures on tongues differently than those who do speak with tongues.

You can find spiritual bigots on both sides of this issue. There are those who will not associate with a believer if he speaks in tongues, but there are also those who will not associate with any believer who doesn't speak in tongues. They are both spiritual bigots, because they elevate themselves above other Christians who think differently than they do.

It's very important to understand that *when a believer is a spiritual bigot, it is because of his attitude, not because of the issue he's intolerant about.* There are churches that speak with tongues who walk in love toward churches that don't, and vice versa.

You see, the Bible says "... endeavoring to keep the unity of the Spirit" (Ephesians 4:3). *Vision unites a church, not doctrine!* Only our simple faith in Jesus Christ as the Lord and Savior of our lives, our common love for Him, and the desire to win souls will bring the Church Body together and cause one local church to walk in love with another local church.

Even within each local church you are going to find many different opinions about the more controversial doctrines, such as end-time prophecy. Satan will try to incite spiritual bigotry over these issues in order to divide the church.

None of these issues even have anything to do with our eternal salvation or the fulfilling of the great commission, however. When we understand this, and we choose to have a love and respect for each believer and maintain a submissive attitude, doctrinal differences cannot affect the unity of the church.

The other area of pride is in natural things, and this is called *prejudice*. One of the most subtle tactics of the devil which prohibits a local body of believers from living together in peace is prejudice toward other believers because of a natural attribute, such as race, color, sex, or social status.

In Galatians 3:28, the Holy Spirit tells us, "There is neither Jew nor Greek, there is neither bond nor free, there is neither male nor female: *for ye are all one in Christ Jesus.*" And whatever is true for the universal Church, is true for the local church.

In the universal Church, God does not recognize race, social class, or sex. Therefore, in the local church, we should not place any significance on these things either. When God looks at us, he sees us as one Body; when we look at our local church, we should see ourselves as one body, also.

In Ephesians 2:11, the Bible says that before we were born again, we were "Gentiles in the flesh." What this is saying is that race and skin color only exist in the flesh, but not in the spirit. God doesn't see us in nationalities. In fact, in heaven He won't put the Jews in one corner and the Greeks in another. We are all one in the Body of Christ.

This verse also says that "there is neither bond nor free," which means that there are no social distinctions in the Body of Christ either. God doesn't favor the rich over the poor; nor does He favor the poor over the rich (see James 2:1-9).

One of my favorite illustrations of our equality in Christ is found in the Old Testament, when David danced before the Lord (Second Samuel 6:15,16). If you recall, the scripture tells us that Michal, David's wife, looked out her window and saw "king David leaping and dancing before the Lord; and she despised him in her heart."

Michal did not despise David just for making a public spectacle of himself. She looked down upon him because he had removed his kingly robes and was parading himself as a common priest. His only garment was the priestly ephod. She despised David for humbling himself before his people, for making the statement that in God there is no class hierarchy, no "bond or free."

Because Michal's security and identity were in natural things instead of spiritual truths, she had loved David because he was the king, not because he was a child of God. She valued him for his position only.

This should not be so in the church. When we walk into the local church, we should be more aware than ever that underneath our lawyer's suit, our welder's clothes, our nurse's uniform, is merely a blood-bought member of the Body of Christ. We need to remove all facades and be who we really are – equal in the sight of God.

It is beautiful to see all kinds of people praising and worshiping God together. A garbage collector turns to give a word of encouragement to a doctor. An engineer prays for a waitress to be healed, while a young college student joins hands with an elderly woman to agree for all her needs to be met.

Lastly, Galatians 3:28 says that in Christ "there is neither male nor female." This means that God makes no distinction between male and female in the Church.

In natural matters, if a woman is married, she is subject to her husband. But where spiritual matters are concerned, she is under the headship of Christ as everyone is in the Body of Christ, men and women alike. Even church history confirms that God moves as mightily through women as He does through men. And Joel prophesied that sons and daughters, servants and handmaids would prophesy (Acts 2:17,18).

Although men and women are both equal in Christ, they are each better suited for particular natural functions in the local church. Deacons and elders can be either male or female, yet I have no female ushers at our church. Ushers may be called on to help handicapped people out of cars, restrain the unruly, carry in chairs or move the pulpit, and men are better suited physically for these jobs.

Women are wonderfully suited to teaching and ministering to children. They exercise much more patience and care for them than many men would. *We have equality in worth, but difference in function.*

More men are called into full-time preaching ministries than women. Is God prejudiced? No, that would be blasphemous. God knows the physical limitations of women and calls them into more supportive roles. Some women are called into preaching ministries, but this is the exception and not the rule. While the number of women called into public ministries in the Bible could be counted on our two hands, they are greatly outnumbered by the men God called from Old Testament to New.

Jesus Himself had no women disciples, most likely because He knew of the hardships and dangers He would face in His travels. However, women were a major financial support of His ministry (Luke 8:2,3). When all of the disciples forsook Him at his arrest and crucifixion, the women remained with Him (Luke 23:49,55), and they later told the disciples of His resurrection (Luke 24:8-10).

I also believe that the office of the pastor is for men only. A woman may stand in that position and do a good job, but she cannot *be* a pastor; in the same way that a woman may be widowed or divorced and have to do the job of a husband, but she cannot *be* a husband.

The main reason I believe this is because the pastor is the head of a local body of believers, just as Jesus is the head of the Body of Christ, and the husband is the head of a family. The Bible likens the relationship between the pastor and his congregation to a marriage. Unlike the other ministry offices, the pastor is "married" to his congregation.

Just as God's ultimate desire is for a man to be the head of every household, I believe it is also His will for a man to be the head of each local church. Women who are single parents will tell you that, through the grace of God, they can provide for their family, train the children up according to the Word of God, and manage to keep the household running smoothly –

128

but it is not God's best! A family and a church need a man as the head.

One issue I will mention here, too, is that often in the local church you will find that certain age groups can be neglected, usually children and senior citizens. They are treated as "second-class citizens" of the Body of Christ. What we need to always remember is that the older saints have the wisdom of living to impart to us, and the young are the spiritual leaders of tomorrow.

Within every children's church are the five-fold ministry gifts, and the elders, bishops, and deacons of your church for the next generation. There should be just as much concern for their spiritual welfare as for the adults'.

In all of these areas – race, social class, sex, and age – the pastor will set the example for the congregation, and then it is up to them to follow. There is nothing more sickening and disheartening than a pastor who favors one race over another, one social class over another, one sex over another, or he ignores the needs of different age groups.

But when the pastor walks in a submissive attitude, with love toward all men and women, and the congregation follows him, a spirit of love and unity holds that church together so tightly that Satan finds no entrance. In this atmosphere of love, faith supernaturally explodes! And that church becomes a powerful tool for God in this earth.

## The Glorious Church

The scriptures remind us again and again that the natural distinctions we must deal with in this earth are temporary. They will perish as we rise to meet Jesus in the air (First Thessalonians 4:16,17)! However, while we are in this flesh, we must handle them *according to the Word of God.*

This means that in any situation, we are to have a submissive attitude. If our boss asks us to perform a task that we love or if he requests that we do something we dislike, we are to cheerfully obey. *Yet, if we are asked to do something that is contrary to the Word of God, we maintain that submissive attitude, but we obey God rather than men.*

Let's illustrate this with the husband and wife again. The wife is equal to the husband in Christ, but her gender places her in submission to her husband. However, if a husband asks his wife never to go to church again, he is violating the Word of God. Submissively, the wife can refuse to obey. In this way, she obeys God rather than men, yet maintains a submissive attitude.

*The submissive attitude brings glory to the Lord Jesus Christ and to His Church.*

First Peter 2:9,10 tells us that the Church is "a chosen generation, a royal priesthood, an holy nation, a peculiar people... which in time past (before we were born again) were not a people, but are now the people of God...."

This verse of scripture declares that the Body of Christ is a completely different nation, a God-made race of people, who are unique in every aspect of their lives. They live for God and love one another as He loves them.

Our purpose is to do God's will in the earth – or, in military terms, we are called to "occupy," – until Jesus, our Leader, returns. It is ironic to the world's way of thinking, but the way the Church "occupies" is to *serve.* In the Kingdom of God, the greatest ruler is the greatest servant.

As the family of God, we are exhorted to "clothe ourselves with humility toward one another," to submit ourselves to those in authority over us, and to "humble ourselves under the mighty hand of God." According to the Bible, *submission is not a place of weakness, it is the place of power.*

First Peter 5:6 says that if we "humble ourselves under the mighty hand of God, He will exalt us *in due time.*" "In due time" means that He will exalt us at just the right moment during our lifetime on earth. We know that the time will come in this life, because *time* will not exist in heaven!

God has appointed times in our lives for the seeds of humility that we have sown to Him to bring forth their harvest of success and fulfillment.  And the degree to which we will be exalted is proportionate to the degree to which we submit ourselves.

*These verses of scripture tell us that the level of our commitment to serve others as though we were serving the Lord Jesus Christ Himself will determine the level of His grace, mercy, and power that operates in our lives.*

When a local body of believers and their pastor begin to walk in "humility of mind," the supernatural unity that is produced gives them the ability to reach their area for Jesus Christ.  They become like one of those brightly lit lampstands of Revelation 1:20, and Jesus is powerfully walking in their midst!

# Chapter Twelve
# How to Know Your Pastor

**And we beseech you, brethren, to know them which labour among you, and are over you in the Lord, and admonish you;**

**And to esteem them very highly in love for their work's sake. And be at peace among yourselves.**

First Thessalonians 5:12,13

IN THE FIRST PART OF First Thessalonians 5:12, the Bible says to *"know* them which labor among you." It is important for the congregation to know the character and beliefs of their pastor.

You might say, "Well, my church is very large, so how can the pastor possibly let everyone get to know him?" The Greek word for "know" in this verse means "to know about," or "to know by observation." It does not indicate an intimate friendship, but a knowledge that you acquire of someone as you watch them from a distance.

Whenever you hear your pastor preach and teach, you are hearing his heart, you are discovering how he thinks and what he believes. And if you want to know what he expects of you, then listen to what he says every time the church doors open, and you'll find out!

Nobody can have more than a few really close friends, especially when you're married and have a family, and the pastor is no exception. You can't expect your pastor to be every member's best friend, but you can get to know him as you listen to his sermons and observe how he handles the challenges of his own life.

## Pastors Are Human

Sometimes church members who don't have a close personal relationship with the pastor tend to believe that he's superhuman, that he doesn't have to deal with the problems that they face everyday. That's why I exhort pastors to be themselves in the pulpit, to let their people see them "at all seasons" (see Chapter Two).

What many believers don't realize is that God calls regular human beings into the ministry, and they are full of mistakes, failures, troubles, and trials just like anybody else. Their calling does not make them immune from the devil, the flesh, or the world.

One time when someone came up to me and said, "You don't deserve to be in the pulpit," I agreed. Then I reminded them that they didn't deserve to be in the congregation, either! All of us are where we are because of the grace of God, and we need to understand this and remind ourselves of it as we submit to those in authority and as we submit to one another.

Years ago, when I first started working for a great man of God whom I highly respected, I was certain that every night God showed him exactly what to do in the ministry, that God gave him policy after policy. But it wasn't long before I saw this man make a mistake, and we had to change policies. Then, a few weeks later, the same thing happened in another area, and we had to change policies again.

I was shocked, but it was then that I learned that even the most spiritual among us are human. I also learned that when a spiritual leader makes a mistake, the believers who follow him make a choice: they will either judge the leader and forsake him, or extend grace to the leader as Jesus extends grace to them when they fail.

Now I'm not talking about persistent sin. If the pastor or a spiritual leader is involved in something immoral or illegal on a regular basis, then that must be disciplined. What I'm referring to here are the everyday errors in judgment that all of us make.

That's why First Thessalonians 5:13 says that the congregation should "esteem them very highly in love for their work's sake." In other words, *you esteem the pastor and love him for the office he stands in, for his preaching and teaching the Word of God, not because he is perfect.*

## Pastors Labor and Admonish

Some church members think that the pastor's job consists of preaching a few sermons a week, counseling a few people, and playing golf or racquetball the rest of the time. I wish! The ministry is work, and the pressures that go with it can be intense.

That's one of the reasons I'm writing this book! There are so many things that God has taught me and shown me from the Word of God over the years that I believe can help other pastors enjoy their calling and increase their effectiveness.

Most of the time, I enjoy praying and studying the Word of God, I love preaching and teaching under the anointing and seeing lives transformed as the people receive from God. Sometimes I am astounded that I get paid for what I love to do!

The problems and the pressures come with people. And there are times I cannot understand why some people do what they do and think what they think! But my job is to love them anyway, to continue to lead them and feed them with the Word of God.

This is where the "admonishing" part of my job enters into the picture. In Hebrews 10:24, the Holy Spirit tells us to "consider one another to *provoke* unto love and to good works."

As a pastor, I am called to admonish the people, which means to put them in remembrance of God's Word. And sometimes this means I must "provoke" the sheep "unto love and good works."

The word "provoke" means "to stimulate or prod," and most of the time this is not a pleasant experience! It's the picture of a cattleman using a sharp cattle prod to jab and poke the cattle again and again. Finally, they become so irritated that they obey him and start moving in the direction they were supposed to be heading in the first place.

When the congregation isn't walking in love or good works in some area, the Holy Spirit has me provoke them with His Word. And if it doesn't work the first time, He'll have me do it again. But the pastor is not the only one who does the provoking!

Hebrews 10:25 goes on to say, "Not forsaking the assembling of ourselves together...but exhorting one another...." The congregation has a responsibility toward each other here, too. If someone in the church sees another member falter in their life of faith or get off into error somewhere, the Holy Spirit will often lead them to "provoke" their friend back to walking in love and good works.

For example, if someone you know in the church becomes offended and begins to harbor a grudge, God may call upon you to humbly remind your friend that in order to continue walking "in love and good works," they must forgive the person who has offended them and give the situation to the Lord.

This doesn't give us a license to go around slapping each other with the Word of God! What these verses of scripture give us is our true responsibility to each other. By "provoking" each other, we eliminate pride, because you cannot go to a brother or sister and "provoke them unto love and good works" if you go to them in arrogance, nor can you be "provoked unto love and good works" by someone else unless you have a submissive attitude.

Once the pastor gives the congregation God's Word on a subject, once he "provokes the congregation unto love and good works," then it's up to the congregation to put that Word into effect in their lives as they live, work and minister together.

The purpose of the pastor is found in Ephesians 4:12: "For the perfecting of the saints, for the work of the ministry, for the edifying of the body of Christ." We have seen in Chapter Four of this book that the primary function of the pastor is to feed the sheep, to preach and teach the Word of God. That is because the more Word the congregation knows and understands, the more confident and bold they are in the world.

The five-fold ministry gifts listed in Ephesians 4:11 are called to perfect the *saints* for the work of the ministry. It is the *congregation* who goes out into the world to be a witness, to preach the gospel to their neighbors and co-workers, to pray for the sick, to bring the Word of God to the streets of their city.

The work of the ministry is not confined to the four walls of the local church; it extends to the highways and byways through the congregation. I admonish my people to take the Word of God that is spoken from the pulpit and apply it to their lives. Resist temptation. Raise up a godly family in a God-rejecting world. Be the best worker in your company. Take your offenses and complaints to the Lord and handle them according to His will. Be a living testimony to the power of the gospel of Jesus Christ.

Again, the pastor can admonish, but he cannot force the congregation to go out and live it. There are times, however, when the Holy Spirit will lead me in a certain direction during the sermon, and I know for certain that one or more of the members of the church are sinning in that area.

As I get off into a certain area, sometimes I can actually see certain people jump or roll their eyes! However, I assure my church that the Holy Spirit tells me *what* to say – He never tells me *who* I'm talking about! *One of the greatest gifts that God has given us in the Body of Christ is privacy.*

The Holy Spirit will step all over the toes of the sinning believer through the Word He leads the pastor to preach, but He will never publicly humiliate someone from the pulpit. I don't know what's going on in the private lives of the members of our church unless they come up and tell me.

I will never forget the time I was teaching in the Book of Proverbs, and the Holy Spirit led me to describe the difference between the "strange woman," who is the prostitute, and the "evil woman," who is the adulteress. The Bible says that the prostitute is just after a man's money, but the adulteress wants to possess his whole life.

As the service closed, a woman came running down the aisle, pointed her finger in my face, and cried, "I'm not after his life! Who told you?" Of course, no one had told me. I never would have known anything if she had remained silent! The old proverb says, "When you throw a rock into a pack of dogs, the one who is hit yells."

Personally, I would rather not know the intimate details of the congregation's lives. I don't want my sermons or my ministry to the people to be tainted because I know certain things about them.

For example, when I pray for someone to be healed, I don't want to be thinking, "Well, they only gave a small amount in the offering last week, and I know that a tenth of their salary would be much more."

I don't want to steer away from certain subjects the Holy Spirit is urging me to cover from the Word of God because I know someone in the congregation will be offended due to the fact that they are involved in that sin or error. On the other hand, I don't want my *flesh* to pressure me to emphasize something because I know someone has sin in their life, either.

It's easier for the pastor to minister in the freedom of the Holy Spirit when he knows little about the private lives of his congregation. If necessary and if possible, the counseling and visitation departments should minister to the people on a more intimate level.

## On a Pedestal

First Thessalonians 5:13 exhorts the members of the congregation to "esteem them (the pastor) very highly in love for their work's sake." The word "esteem" means to "consider," and this verse says to "consider them very highly." In other words, the people should put their pastor on a pedestal.

The word "work's" refers to everything the pastor gives to the congregation and the fruit that is produced through his ministry. The pastor is to be put on a pedestal and to be loved by his people because of the work, the production, he does in their behalf.

This verse is saying that you should *honor your pastor because of what he does and because he stands in the office of a pastor, not because of his personality.* If he tells great jokes, is very friendly, and loves dogs and children, that's fine. But if he is quiet, keeps to himself, and chooses to remain single, you should still respect him and submit to him for the spiritual guidance and teaching he brings to your life.

When I first took the church I pastor now, the car I owned was a TransAm. One of the members of the congregation came to me and told me that they did not think that this was the kind of car a pastor should drive, that it would offend people, and that I should get something else.

I told them, "I've found that no car manufacturer makes "pastors' cars," and I like this one. It meets my needs." Because I would not exchange my car for the kind of car they thought I should drive, they left the church.

Can you imagine that person, standing before Jesus, and Jesus asking them, "Why did you leave the church I called you to?" They would have to reply, "Because the pastor drove a TransAm!"

You might find this silly and amusing, but unfortunately this sort of thing happens in churches all the time. People will get born again in a church, their lives will be changed, their families restored, and one day they are offended and leave the church because the pastor has made a decision or set a policy that does not agree with them. The new building has chairs instead of pews, or the new carpet is blue instead of red, or the pastor got a more expensive house than they have.

I often wonder, when Satan attacks their health or their family or their job, will they look him boldly in the eye and declare, "I rebuke you, Satan, because we have traditional pews and plush blue carpet!"

If you submit to the leadership of a pastor and commit yourself to a local body of believers, eventually you will be offended or disappointed in some way. As you get to know your pastor better, you will have to go through the process of having him fall off of the pedestal as his faults, weaknesses, and personality become known, and then putting him back up there by the Word and God's grace!

I can almost guarantee that the devil will make sure that whatever things hurt or offend you will be done to you by someone in the church, usually by someone you would least expect, and possibly even by the pastor himself.

If the believer doesn't handle the offense according to the Word of God, then everything they see will be colored by their hurt or anger. Suddenly, the pastor doesn't seem to be anointed anymore. Close friends in the congregation are excited about the sermon or coming events in the church, but they sound stupid to the one who has been offended. Finally, the offense grows to the degree that nothing satisfies them.

Until they ask God to forgive them and rid themselves of bitterness and resentment, the offended believer will be miserable. Basically, their pride is separating them from fellowship with God and their brothers and sisters in Christ.

There are also going to be decisions and policies coming down from leadership that will displease you, and when you make your opinion known, those in authority may not see it your way in the end. But these are not valid reasons for leaving a church.

Believers may leave a church because the leadership has gotten into habitual and unrepented sin or heretical teaching of the Word of God, not because the pastor's wife sings the solo every Sunday or the offering is collected in buckets instead of brass plates!

The believer who storms out of the church because of an offense or a difference of opinion should ask themselves these important questions: Is the pastor preaching and teaching the Word of God? Are people being born again, filled with the Spirit, and restored to fellowship with the Lord? Is the congregation prospering and growing in the things of God? Are families being strengthened? And most important, is this where God wants me to be?

These are the important issues in the local church. And when the congregation esteems the pastor and church leadership "for their work's sake," First Thessalonians 5:6 goes on to say that they will *"be at peace among themselves."*

## The Bond of Peace

When a pastor and his congregation live in peace, there is no way that Satan can get his foot in the door, and there is no limit to what God can do. But peace is not something that just drops out of heaven for no reason. Peace is something you do battle to maintain.

The greatest leaders of nations will tell you that in order to live in peace, they must maintain a strong military defense. And sometimes, in order to stay free and keep the peace, a war must be fought. In Ephesians 4:1-3, Paul exhorts us:

> **I therefore, the prisoner of the Lord, beseech you that ye walk worthy of the vocation wherewith ye are called,**

> **With all lowliness and meekness, with longsuffering, forbearing one another in love;**

> **Endeavoring to keep the unity of the Spirit in the bond of peace.**

We are unified *spiritually* because we are born again, but Paul is urging us to allow this spiritual unity to extend into the *natural realm* – where we live with one another. This is the battle that we wage to maintain peace in our lives and in our churches. The essence of unity manifests when we walk in love toward one another.

Walking in unity with God is not as difficult as walking in unity with each other. Verse 3 says that walking in unity with each other is an "endeavor," it is work! I know God loves me, and I know that I can count on Him, but I'm not so sure about other people!

That's why many Christians stay home and watch Christian television instead of coming to church and getting involved. The difficult part of the Christian life is rubbing shoulders with other believers, each with their own set of problems, and submitting to a pastor who is less than perfect.

"How can I praise the Lord with Sister So-And-So's loud voice blasting in my ear? Every time we have praise and worship, she is so off-key, she gives a whole new meaning to 'make a joyful noise!' And I just know that Brother What's-His-Name will sit by me and ask me to join the choir again. And I really wish that family would discipline their children – honestly, they are tearing up the Sunday school rooms!"

In the verses of scripture above, Paul describes the battle to keep the "unity of the Spirit" as walking "worthy of the vocation wherewith ye are called (being faithful on the job), with all lowliness (humility, a submissive attitude) and meekness (a teachable heart), with longsuffering (patience), forbearing (or putting up with) one another in love."

It takes effort to walk in love, but the result is to live in peace and unity in the Body of Christ. This is one of the special blessings that come with being a member of God's family. Only believers can enjoy the "unity of the Spirit" which comes from walking in love, because the Bible says that the "love of God is shed abroad in our hearts by the Holy Ghost which is given to us" (Romans 5:5).

The world can come together against a common enemy or in a common cause, they can sign a temporary truce in war, but they will never have peace or unity, because peace and unity, which come from walking in love toward one another, come from the Holy Spirit.

Most importantly, there is a supernatural power that accompanies the "unity of the Spirit." In Matthew 18:19,20

Jesus says that, "if two of you shall agree on earth as touching any thing that they shall ask, it shall be done for them of my Father which is in heaven. For where two or three are gathered together in my name, there am I in the midst of them." Jesus, the High Priest of the Church, walks in the midst of us *when we agree.* When we agree, the miracle-working power of God is released!

Jesus is not commanding us to agree about our doctrines; He is telling us to agree in prayer about a need so that the need can be met. Many believers think that the ultimate sign of maturity in the Christian life is faith. But faith is only the beginning. The ultimate sign of maturity in the Christian life is love, *agape love.* This is the God kind of love. "But God commendeth his love toward us, in that, while we were yet sinners, Christ died for us" (Romans 5:8).

*Love will put aside personal differences to see someone saved, healed, and set free.* Ephesians 4:3 says that the unity of the Spirit is kept in the bond of peace. The "bond of peace" is the believer's commitment to choose to walk in love toward other believers regardless of the challenges raised by the world, the devil, or the flesh.

While we are on this earth, the Church will never walk in the unity of doctrines, traditions, politics, or personal preferences. But we can overcome our differences and achieve "unity of the Spirit in the bond of peace." When the Holy Spirit is allowed to reign in our lives, "the love of God is shed abroad in our hearts," and we can walk in love toward one another. This is the bond of peace in action.

You can submit to your pastor, love him, "esteem him highly for his work's sake," and still not agree with everything he preaches and teaches. And you can rub shoulders with the most *unusual* people, pray with them, and see God move mountains. How? By "endeavoring (choosing to walk in love) to keep the unity of the Spirit in the bond of peace."

Because the explosive supernatural power of God is present when a pastor and his congregation lives in unity and peace, the Church is constantly being bombarded by Satan's attacks. Satan knows that if he can divide us, particularly if he can incite the flesh to rise up in strife and contention, we are powerless. He also knows that if we stand together in love, we can take the gospel to the world.

Unity and peace are established in the local church by the heart of the pastor. The bond of peace, or the commitment to walk in love toward others, must begin with leadership.

We have seen that you can know your pastor by his *works*, and "esteem him highly for his work's sake," which is to labor in the Word of God and prayer and to admonish the people. This is how you know his *beliefs*. But of equal importance is to know your pastor's *character*.

You know a person's character by observing the manifestation of the fruit of the Spirit in their life. Galatians 5:22,23 names these godly character traits as love, joy, peace, longsuffering (patience), gentleness, goodness (purity), faith (faithfulness), meekness (teachable attitude), and temperance (self-control).

Jesus also said that you would know them by their fruit, which is another reference to the fruit of the Spirit listed above.

> For every tree is known by his own fruit. For of thorns men do not gather figs, nor of a bramble bush gather they grapes.

> A good man out of the good treasure of his heart bringeth forth that which is good; and an evil man out of the evil treasure of his heart bringeth forth that which is evil: for of the abundance of the heart his mouth speaketh.

> **Luke 6:44,45**

How can you love, esteem, and submit to your pastor and still have major differences in various areas? Because you know his character. You see the fruit of the Spirit in his life. His heart is after God, his desire is to serve God and the people, he loves his congregation and prays for them, he is faithful to study and teach the Word of God and then live it to the best of his ability, and there is a consistent stability and joy in his life because of these things.

Therefore, you know your pastor by listening to his sermons and observing his manner of life. These things reveal his beliefs and his character.

The relationship between a pastor and his congregation is very special. God gives the pastor a love for his people that sees beyond their weaknesses and failures to all they can be in Christ. His every effort is focused on helping them to grow spiritually, encouraging them to know their God more intimately through the Holy Spirit, and giving them the knowledge and wisdom from God's Word to live fulfilled, prosperous lives.

When a congregation knows that their pastor is committed to them, that he will walk in love toward them and be a faithful example for them, they will easily accept his leadership, commit themselves to be a part of the ministry of the church, and begin to walk in love toward each other.

The Bible says that faith worketh by love (Galatians 5:6), and faith is the supernatural power by which mountains are removed and captives set free. But the trigger for this vast power is love. When a pastor chooses to love his congregation in word and deed, and the congregation responds by following his example, the local church becomes an awesome powerhouse through which God can reach a generation for Jesus Christ.

Like the church at Ephesus, a pastor and congregation who commit themselves to keep the faith and walk in love can bring the mighty, healing hands of Jesus to the broken and hurting people in their community. And it is through great local churches, who know God's Word and how to walk by the Spirit, that God can move mightily in cities, in nations, and throughout the world.

Bob Yandian is pastor of Grace Fellowship in Tulsa, Oklahoma. His anointed teaching ministry, boldly proclaiming the uncompromised Word of God, is founded on Isaiah 33:6: "Wisdom and knowledge are the stability of our times and strength of salvation."

When he was called to the ministry, Bob left Oklahoma State University to attend Trinity Bible College, whose director and founder, Charles Duncombe, travelled with Smith Wigglesworth. After graduating from Bible school, he studied Greek at Southwestern College in Oklahoma City.

As a founding member of Grace Fellowship, Bob began teaching various Sunday school classes, and one grew to over 200 in attendance. He was employed by Kenneth Hagin Ministries as Tape Production Manager in 1973, and this led to his becoming an instructor at Rhema Bible Training Center in 1977. Soon after that, he was appointed Dean of Instructors at Rhema, but he resigned in 1980 to become Pastor of Grace Fellowship. Under his leadership, the church has grown from 1,200 to 3,000.

Bob not only ministers the Word of God to his congregation, but he teaches at Grace Fellowship's School of the Local Church and hosts his Pastors' Conference every January. He and his wife, Loretta, live in Tulsa with their two children, Lori and Robb.

# Books by Bob Yandian

**JOEL**
*The Outpouring of God's Glory*

**GALATIANS**
*The Spirit-Controlled Life*

**PROVERBS**
*Principles of Wisdom*

**EPHESIANS**
*The Maturing of the Saints*

**RESURRECTION**
*Our Victory Over Death*

**DECENTLY AND IN ORDER**
*A Guide to New Testament Church Government*

**SALT AND LIGHT**
*Sermon on the Mount*

**OIL AND WINE**
*The Indwelling and Infilling of the Holy Spirit*

**ONE NATION UNDER GOD**
*The Rise or Fall of a Nation*

**CALLING AND SEPARATION**
*Opening the Door to Your Ministry*